Interviews With Legendary Writers From Beyond

Cathy McGough

Stratford Living Publishing

This updated version published in September 2023.

Previously published as ISBN:13: 978-14796781 on Create Space Platform in 2013.

Library of Congress Control Number 2003112317.

ISBN: 978-1-990332-03-6

What Readers Are Saying...

“Read this book and by so doing, add another dimension to your pleasure and the works of these great authors. By careful research, and some soul-searching imagination Cathy McGough brings them all to life. Having read this book, the reader will always have the impression of being in touch with the words of their favourite writer. They will not just be reading his work but enjoying that extra dimension: the feeling of being read to.”

A. R. (David) Lewis, Author of: “The Cup and Saucer Tree” and “A Field of Red Poppies.”

"I grew up enjoying the heartfelt writings of these poets and authors! Many times have I wished I could have gotten to know them as the people themselves outside their words across paper. Cathy McGough made this happen!"

Amazon Reviewer

"I loved the interview format, and the bits and pieces of poet's and authors' lives that I never knew about. I loved the funny interim pieces with Madame Delatour and the narrator. Although I'd come across and read almost all the authors/poets in this book, I learned something new or amusing about each of them and I actually found one I WANT to read!"

Amazon Reviewer

“A charming and engaging collection of author biographies. Cathy McGough introduces the great ones with the help of psychic, Madame Delatour. Each interview snaps with the electricity of a séance as the ethers open to reveal another author returning for a friendly chat. Cathy captures the essence of the writers, bringing forth their strengths along with their vulnerabilities. Each entity is obviously familiar and dear to her heart. This book is a must-read to learn about famous authors in a memorable way or just simply to celebrate them."

Jo Janoski, Author of: “Tea and Chocolates” and “Faithful.” Photographer, Janoski Studio Pittsburgh Photography

"The writer did an incredible amount of research into the lives and writings of eminent poets and writers and presented it in an intelligent way including fictional interviews and engaging collection of writings. The humourous presentation of anecdotes captured my imagination and attention from start to finish."

Amazon Reviewer

"A delightful primer for any reader interested in getting to know some of the world's greatest English language writers. Full of painstakingly researched historical facts, the humorous delivery and surprising anecdotes kept me turning the pages. Another thing I really appreciated were the physical descriptions of the author. From Stephen Leacock's humour to the inspiration of Rudyard Kipling, th is book was a fabulous read."

Amazon Reviewer

“A blend of history and literature. Cathy McGough’s unique style captures your imagination. She takes you to the realm of the greatest authors the world has known. It is an adventure you will not forget."

Walter L. Jones, Owner of Jones Outlet

"An excellent job transforming the biographies of iconic literary names into an interesting and incredible collection. It was a fun read that captured my imagination and held my attention all the way through. Recommended to every bookworm!"

Amazon Reviewer

"A lot of hard work went into this book. I especially liked the Edgar Allan Poe interview. This would be useful for high school students to help them to learn about the giants of the literary world."

Amazon Reviewer

"I am a poet, so I appreciated Ms McGough has placed such a prominent place for poets in this book that uses humour to highlight these "legendary writers."

Amazon Reviewer

"A must read for all who are genuine literary lovers!"

Amazon Reviewer

Contents

Introduction

"This book will make a traveller of thee."
John Bunyan. The Pilgrim's Progress

Dear **Readers,**

I would like to take this opportunity to personally thank two of my favourite high school teachers. They are Mr. Mavor and Mr. Hurley. Both at Central Secondary High School, in Stratford, Ontario, Canada. Between the two of them, they introduced me to the writings of many of the writers I've interviewed for my book.

I'd be amiss if I did not also lend a thanks to The Stratford Festival. Having the opportunity to see LIVE THEATRE right on my doorstep for entire life has been a privilege and an honour.

I hope you'll enjoy reading my interviews, as much as I enjoyed writing them!

Happy Reading!
Cathy McGough
Your Interviewer of Legendary Writers From Beyond

Foreword

BY CHRISTOPHER INGHAM

It is a sad comment upon the state of contemporary writing on literature that one seldom comes across critical or biographical texts that reflect the unbounded joy that those of us fortunate enough to be adolescents in the 1960s experienced when we first discovered writers of the calibre of Dickens, Wilkie Collins, Dostoevsky, Coleridge, and Poe.

With the possible exception of Harold Bloom, so much writing on what those of us who are politically incorrect like to term "great literature" appears to be ideologically based.

One suspects that modern critics are so straitjacketed by the demands of current academic orthodoxy that they have either lost the capacity to delight in the works of "legendary writers" or they are too afraid to allow themselves to be immersed in the imaginative worlds created by these writers. Similarly, it would appear that biographers also feel the need to place the lives of these writers into some sort of ideological context that supposedly informs their writing to such an extent that the imaginative power of their art is often devalued.

Having become so cynical about the nature of contemporary critical and biographical responses to "legendary writers", particularly those of the 19th century, I was pleasantly surprised when I stumbled across Cathy McGough's fascinatingly titled work "Interviews With Legendary Writers from Beyond."

Here, at last, was a writer who is not afraid to share her delight in the lives and works of those who have so obviously provided her with pleasure throughout her reading life. I began by and understanding of each of her subjects that I read the book from cover to cover in little over a single sitting.

Whilst there are many wonderful aspects to this book, I must comment upon three that stand out. Firstly, the technique of using Madame Delatour, a Medium, as a means Interviews With Legendary Writers From Beyond of bringing these writers to life works extremely well and given the interest of Victorians in spiritualism this technique adds another dimension to the work.

Secondly is the fact that Cathy's imaginative interaction with the writers in parts of the world that are real and important to her, helps create a sense of immediacy that is crucial in bringing these figures from the past to life.

Thirdly, and most importantly, is the way in which by encouraging the writers to not only talk about themselves and their writing, but to also read and introduce parts of their work, Cathy has found a way to introduce her readers to works of each writer with which they may not be familiar. In addition, her provision of a list of her favourite works by each writer should encourage the reader to explore some of those works.

I believe that this book will be a most valuable reference for not only teachers and students but also for those readers who have missed out on the works of these "legendary writers" in the past and who may now be encouraged to share Cathy's delight and enthusiasm for the creative genius of these extraordinary writers. I will certainly be recommending this book to my Year 11 and Year 12 literature students.

I cannot close this Foreword without extolling Cathy to expand and extend this book by interviewing writers such asThomas Hardy, D. H. Lawrence, the Bronte sisters, and Jane Austen. Of course, even more fascinating would be a meeting between Robert Browning, who was so sceptical of spiritualism that he wrote that wonderful poem Mr. Sludge,

'The Medium.' A meeting between Browning, Cathy and Madame Delatour would be fascinating.

Christopher Ingham M Ed., B Ed., TSTC
Head of English at The Hamilton and Alexandra College, Victoria, Australia, and
a Poet in his spare time.

Chapter One

GETTING TO KNOW YOUR MEDIUM

As we are embarking on this adventure together it is most appropriate for us to include an interview with the person who helped to make this book possible: my friend Madame Delatour.

You may ask why you haven't seen Madame Delatour before, and perhaps wonder why we didn't take the opportunity presented to us through this book by including a photograph of her.

Alas, that is not possible. For Madame Delatour's "gift" makes her un-photogenic. In fact, she may lose some or all her powers if anyone flashes her. Therefore, please keep your cameras away in her presence ladies and gentlemen.

And speaking of gentlemen, many who have read part of this book in the form of a column (not to mention at least one of our Legendary Writers from Beyond) have asked – if our Madame Delatour is married or attached in any way. I assure you she is single.

Madame Delatour was born on December 31, 1950, in Paris, France. She has never been married and is seeking a partner who will not be jealous of her special abilities. She has a soft spot for men with Scottish accents (as you will see for yourself when we meet with Robbie Burns.) If you would like to correspond with Madame Delatour, please do so via our Publisher. Attach a photo of yourself, as well as a certified copy of your net worth. Madame Delatour will only respond to those gentlemen who have "The Right Stuff."

First, I must note, Madame Delatour and I had words regarding the venue for our interview. I suggested my humble abode since it was good enough for Shelley, Coleridge, Longfellow and others, but she thought my idea was preposterous. She wanted to be pampered, thus I decided to splash out!

At this very moment, we are revolving around the City of Sydney, Australia, relaxing in its posh and elegant (not to mention expensive) restaurant called "Centrepoint," which is appropriately named for its location.

Madame Delatour is dressed to the nines for the occasion. She is wearing a swishy gold lamé evening gown with hundreds, perhaps thousands of mirror-ball type sequins, and a pair of black patent leather shoes with three-inch heels. She is sporting large gold dangly earrings and several bracelets upon each wrist. Madame Delatour towers over me, since I am only 5 ft. 4 in., to her barefoot 5 ft. 8 in.

As we walk towards our table it isn't surprising that everyone turns around to gaze at us. Madame Delatour's earrings and bracelets make their usual music in tune with our steps as we are escorted to our table. We take our seats relatively quickly and sigh in unison, as we look down upon Sydney in all its night-time glory.

Lights twinkle as far as the eye can see and all around us the stars join in, seeming to compete with earth's lights to see which are the brightest. Madame Delatour (or Blanchetta as we shall call her henceforth) proceeds to order not one, but two Mai Tai's both of which are for her own consumption. I order a Black Russian and then our interview begins.

Q: Blanchetta, how did you first discover your unique "gift?"

A: I first discovered it when I was four years old. My Grandfather bought me a tricycle and he used to push me as I rode upon it, and together we would laugh and play. It was a very special time and I loved him dearly. Every time I would ring the golden bell he attached to the handlebars, he would shout "Look out everyone, Etta is coming!" Etta was his special name for me.

Shortly after I had my fourth birthday party, my Grandfather died. After that, I refused to go anywhere near my tricycle. My parents tried everything to encourage me to ride, since they knew I had loved it so, but I could not. I would not. (Even as a small child, I was very strong willed and stubborn when it suited me.) In this case, without my Grandfather, the tricycle lost all its purpose.

One afternoon, I was in the backyard and it began spitting. I did not want to go inside. My tricycle was sitting in the yard, and it looked lonely without me. I didn't want it to get wet. I was afraid the rain might hurt the bell. I knew for certain my Grandfather would not approve of my negligence.

So, I began pushing it, and soon the tears began to stream down my face. I missed my Grandfather and longed to hear him call my name. No one called me "Etta" anymore. It was like a part of me had died with him.

Grandfather always made time for me and without him, I felt lonely. I looked up at the sky, and defiantly rang the bell. I rang it and rang it as the tears streamed down my face. The raindrops joined in almost like they knew how lonely and miserable my life was without him.

Suddenly, his hands were on my shoulders and he said, "Look out everyone, Etta is coming!" and I was ringing the bell and he was pushing me, and we were laughing and playing, and the rain was coming down harder and harder.

Blanchetta removed a tissue from her handbag, and daintily patted the tears from her eyes. She performed a rather tuba-like nose blow, so loudly that everyone turned their heads towards us and stared. I perused the room, fighting back the tears while patting Blanchetta's hand. She was inconsolable; thus, I ordered another Mai Tai. Blanchetta tossed it back and then continued with her story.

I knew then, that I had a special gift. Yet I was afraid what would happen if I told anyone, so I kept it a secret.

Q: Did you ever use your "gift" to help with homework and exams?

A: Yes, I must admit I did. My first experience in reading one of William Shakespeare's plays was dans L 'Ecole. "As You Like It" was the play our teacher chose, and I could not figure it out for the life of me. Why our curriculum included such a difficult play I shall never know.

So, I contacted "The Bard" himself to be my own personal tutor. I told him about the problems I was having in understanding "As You Like It" – and Mr. Shakespeare became Jacques, reciting his soliloquy with passion. I can still see him before me today:

AS YOU LIKE IT

Act II, Scene VII
All the world's a stage,
And all the men and women merely players;
They have their exits and their entrances,
And one man in his time plays many parts,
His acts being seven ages. At first, the infant,
Mewling and puking in the nurse's arms.
Then the whining schoolboy, with his satchel
And shining morning face, creeping like snail
Unwillingly to school. And then the lover,
Sighing like furnace, with a woeful ballad
Made to his mistress' eyebrow. Then a soldier,

Full of strange oaths and bearded like the pard
Jealous in honour, sudden and quick in quarrel,
Seeking the bubble reputation
Even in the canon's mouth. And then the justice,
In fair round belly with good capon lined,
With eyes severe and beard of formal cut,
Full of wise saws and modern instances;
And so, he plays his part. The sixth age shifts
Into the lean and slippered pantaloon
With spectacles on nose and pouch on side;
His youthful hose, well saved, a world too wide
For his shrunk shank, and his big manly voice,
Turning again towards childish treble, pipes
And whistles in his sound. Last scene of all,
That ends this strange eventful history,
Is second childishness and mere oblivion,
Sans teeth, sans eyes, sans taste, sans everything. (1)

Madame Delatour's soliloquy evoked a standing ovation from the crowd. As she descended from the tabletop she bowed to her audience. The waiter arrived with a bottle of Dom Perignon and popped the cork as the applause continued. Together Madame Delatour and I raised our glasses in appreciation of the gift donated by a fellow diner and the interview continued.

After Mr. Shakespeare finished his recitation – I GOT IT! As well as being a successful playwright and poet, Mr. Shakespeare also had hidden talents for acting. He implored me to see his work live – whenever possible – in order to fully appreciate it.

I explained how his works were still performed live all over the world. He seemed well pleased about his longevity and then I mentioned the debates over the years concerning the authorship of his works. He did not seem surprised by some of the false allegations but was truly astounded when I revealed the supposition that his dear wife Anne Hathaway penned them.

Besides Mr. Shakespeare, I met and spoke with Albert Einstein, Alexander Graham Bell, Mahatma Gandhi, Winston Churchill, and countless others. As time moved on, I came to understand, through planning and concentration that I could keep my guests for a little bit longer with every contact I made. The maximum amount of time I can hang onto a guest for today is thirty minutes.

Q: Did you ever fall in love with any of those whom you contacted?

A: One morning in 1972, I woke up and Jim Morrison, that gorgeous man who was lead singer for "The Doors" was in bed beside me! Yes, it is true!

He was lying there, naked from the waist up (and I wasn't sure what state he was in under the covers!) He was staring at the ceiling, with both of his arms cradling his head and singing "Riders in the storm, riders in the storm, into this world we're born, into this world we're thrown, like a dog without a bone, an actor without a home, riders on the storm." (2)

At first, I was too shocked to say anything. I modestly snuggled the covers up all around my neck blushing furiously.

Jim rolled over onto his side, leaned on his elbow and stopped singing in mid-sentence. He looked deeply into my eyes. My heart fluttered like a bird in a cage. He said, "I think you have a question or two for me?"

I racked my brain to think of something to say, but my mind was blank. I blurted out something, something which made absolutely no sense at all and he promptly tossed off the covers and stood up (he was wearing black pants thank God!)

He began jumping up and down on my bed singing "Hello, I love you won't you tell me your name, Hello I love you let me jump on your game." (3)

I thought the roof was going to cave in (not to mention my bed!) I heard my mother and father shouting downstairs "Arret Arret! Blanchetta Arret!"

Jim just kept singing and jumping, like a child on a trampoline. I was laughing hysterically and crying at the same time. I sat frozen like a deer caught in headlights when I heard my mother and father coming up the stairs. Once they got to my door the pounding started. (Fortunately, I always locked my bedroom door at night.)

Jim waved, jumped as high as he could jump and disappeared into the ceiling. I have never forgotten our meeting and have loved him ever since. I often watch reruns of his appearance on "The Ed Sullivan Show" and my heart gets all a flutter once again. That is the worst thing about my "gift."

Q: Do you mean – once you bring someone back to earth, you can never get in contact with him or her again?

A: Sometimes, as I pass from time period to time period, people on the other side try to grab my attention. Imagine, you are swirling through the ages, and various dead people, sometimes evil, sometimes good and almost always very famous – are grabbing at you, trying to grasp onto your coattails. Trying to force you to take them with you so they might have the opportunity to enter this life again – even if it is just for a few minutes.

Q: Sometimes evil? Please explain!

A: I shudder to think of the time when Jack the Ripper grabbed hold of me and tried to make his way through the time portal into the present. I had been setting up an appointment for an interview with Lord Tennyson, when Jack so rudely interrupted and tried to sabotage the process. I had to sever contact with Mr. Tennyson, and fight to keep Jack from taking control. He was stronger than I ever could have imagined. It took everything I possessed to shake him off.

My mind wandered back to that day when Madame Delatour fainted. Only smelling salts brought her back to us. When she came around, she was shaking from head to toe. Two large Chivas Regals – neat helped to calm her nerves. After a little self-medicating she insisted on trying to contact Lord Tennyson once again.

I protested, saying we should wait until she had ample time to recover, but Blanchetta exclaimed, "Jack the Ripper caused enough panic in his day to last a lifetime and he will not terrorize the future." The interview with Lord Tennyson went on without a hitch.

Q: One poet seems to speak to you quite frequently: Lord Byron. Has he been in contact lately?

A: Oh yes, my yes. If I don't have anyone to contact, then he contacts me. He is anxiously awaiting your interview. He has much to say and understands we must prioritize interviews by request. He is very flirtatious and will prove to be an interesting subject.

Q: Would you like to tell everyone how we met Blanchetta?

A: You were in France, at The Eiffel Tower. The year was 1996. You were on a journey to rediscover your Muse. I was trying to escape from my "gift." We met at The Eiffel Tower and talked for quite some time. I tried to help you by quoting a poem from Charles Baudelaire:

Nothing exists without a purpose.
Therefore, my existence has purpose. What purpose?
I do not know.
It is not I therefore who assigned it.
It is therefore someone more learned than I am.
Therefore, I must pray for that someone to enlighten me.
That is the wisest resolution. (4)

As I spoke, Charles Baudelaire appeared. After that, you and I became friends. We wrote to each other, always talking about poetry and writers and literature.

In the end, we decided to invite the world to share our Interviews with Legendary Writers from Beyond. That is how the idea for this book was conceived.

At that moment, our food arrived and so our interview came to an abrupt end. Even so, I do hope you enjoyed meeting Madame Delatour.

Bon Appetit!

Cathy McGough
Your Interviewer of Legendary Writers From Beyond

Chapter Two

LORD TENNYSON AND ME

This chapter is dedicated to my dear Grandmother Mabel Cahill introduced me to Tennyson's poetry.

Good morning all! Today, we are going to be honoured with a visit from our very special guest Alfred, Lord Tennyson who will soon be joining us!

Lord Tennyson was born in 1809 and lived until 1892. At the tender age of thirty-three, he was as famous as a rock star or a movie actor is today. He received letters from women all over the world, young and old – women who were enamoured by his masterful use of the English language (not to mention his handsome appearance.)

But it wasn't just the women, who loved the works of Lord Tennyson. Imagine young soldiers, reciting this poem, as they were being led into battle:

THE CHARGE OF THE LIGHT BRIGADE
Half a league, half a league,
Half a league onward,

All in the valley of Death
Rode the six hundred.
'Forward, the Light Brigade!
Charge for the guns!' he said:
Into the valley of Death
Rode the six hundred.
'Forward, the Light Brigade!'
Was there man dismay'd?
Not tho' the soldier knew
Someone had blunder'd:
Theirs not to make reply,
Theirs not to reason why,
Theirs but to do and die:
Into the valley of Death
Rode the six hundred.
Cannon to the right of them,
Cannon to the left of them,
Cannon in front of them
Volley'd and thunder'd
Storm'd at with shot and shell
Boldly they rode and well,
Into the jaws of Death,
Into the mouth of Hell
Rode the six hundred.
Flash'd all their sabers bare,
Flash'd as they turn'd in air,
Sabring the gunners there,
Charging an army, while
All the world wonder'd:
Plunged in the battery-smoke
Right thro' the line they broke;
Cossack and Russian
Reel'd from the saber-stroke
Shatter'd and sunder'd.
Then they rode back, but not,

Not the six hundred.
Cannon to the right of them,
Cannon to the left of them,
Cannon behind them
Volley'd and thunder'd;
Storm'd at with shot and shell,
While horse and hero fell,
They that had fought so well
Came thro' the jaws of Death
Back from the mouth of Hell,
All that was left of them,
Left of six hundred.
When can their glory fade?
O the wild charge they made!
All the world wonder'd.
Honour the charge they made!
Honour the Light Brigade,
Noble six hundred! (1)

If you still have doubts, concerning the power of Lord Tennyson's writing, then move closer and I will tell you a tale about him you will never forget!

Picture this: A Military Captain in the British Army hastily tucking away a copy of Lord Tennyson's poems into the breast pocket of his uniform, then rushing onto the battlefield where he is shot. He falls onto the ground, clutching his chest and waiting for the pain. Nothing happens. He reaches into his pocket, pulls out the book and discovers a bullet lodged in its cover.

Would it be wrong to say then, that Lord Tennyson's words saved a man's life? I don't think so!

Lord Tennyson lived in Epping Forest, England and his preferred time of the day was early morning when he would take a solitary walk. I'm hoping he won't mind if I join him today as we stroll around the stunning Cooks River.

Since Lord Tennyson will not be properly attired to be seen in public when he arrives, I have taken the liberty of purchasing a tracksuit for him from St. Vincent de Paul's second-hand shop. I have also managed to get a pair of Adidas and Nike runners along with a "just in case" pair of Jesus sandals from our local Salvation Army store.

At precisely 7 a.m., Madame Delatour stood up, waving her arms around while her robes floated, and her earrings jangled like wind chimes. Once she recovered from the before mentioned hi-jacking incident (re: Jack the Ripper) it didn't take long before she was able to contact Lord Tennyson. I waited anxiously for him to materialise – still fascinated by the process –

When lo and behold Lord Tennyson - who is perhaps the greatest lyric poet who ever lived - was standing before me.

He was tall, and I could see why he had been compared to both Hercules and Apollo. (2) His eyes were warm, in the shade of walnuts. He had a long-distinguished nose and curly thick hair - which Delilah would have loved to get her hands on. He was attired in a long black waistcoat, black pants, high boots, and a grey cravat. He had a calm elegance about him, which made me feel like curtseying. When I extended my hand to him, he kissed it gently and then did the same to Madame Delatour's hand. Lord Tennyson was quite the charmer.

I explained my idea - to join him in a morning stroll - and asked if he would mind changing into an appropriate costume for the year 2002. He agreed with enthusiasm.

When he re-joined us, the transformation was quite astonishing. Lord Tennyson looked rather dapper in his new duds. He commented on the softness of the fabrics and said he felt comfortable dressed in his new attire. The tracksuit and the Jesus sandals fit him like a charm.

I pushed the remote-control garage door opener as we walked down the stairs and into our dark garage. Lord Tennyson exclaimed loudly "The Heavens are moving!" when he saw the door rising like a curtain, inviting us to explore Sydney. When we reached the middle of the garage, Lord Tennyson took several minutes to examine our Honda Legend, asking questions as to its purpose. I promised if we had time, we could go for a spin.

Before we exited the garage, Lord Tennyson made a request. He wanted to open and close the garage door again. I let him, but only once - after all, he was aristocracy - then we were on our way.

Q: Many great writers were your friends like: Carlyle, Swinburne, Eliot, and Emerson. Name a writer you didn't meet, but wish you had?

A: I never met Lord Byron. I was fifteen when the news of his death came like a terrible catastrophe to darken that joyous morning of my life. On a rock near my family home in the little Village of Somersby, I recall carving an epitaph, which read: "BYRON IS DEAD." (3)

Q: I have heard some remarkable stories regarding your work, especially "In Memoriam" which you wrote to commemorate the death of your best friend and fellow poet Arthur Hallam. You must have been pleased when Queen Victoria read it.

A: Yes, Queen Victoria received a copy of my book when she was in the midst of her grief at the loss of The Duke of Wellington. I am told her tears fell upon many a line of my work as she read and that my words comforted her. The Little Lady of Windsor made me a great honour by appointing me Poet Laureate. I smiled and observed "Why should I be selfish and not suffer an honour to be done to literature in my name?" (4)

At this point in our walk, we were approaching the children's park, and many were running up and down the slippery dips, swinging and climbing on the jungle gyms. Parents looked on supervising and chatting. Lord Tennyson asked if we could stop to watch, thus we took to a park bench.

Q: What is your favourite childhood memory?

A: I was perhaps five years old, when the March English wind was sweeping along the garden. I remember rushing headlong at the elements, waving my hands and screaming, "I hear a voice that is speaking in the storm!" It was a feeling of power that someone or something was attempting to communicate with me. I never felt such elation. (5)

Q: I know spirituality played a very large part in your life. Could you tell me what Jesus Christ means to you?

A: What the sun is to that flower Jesus Christ is to me. I am amazed at the splendour of Christ's purity and holiness, and at His infinite beauty. (6)

Q: Might I convince you to recite a poem for me?

A: Convince? My dear lady, try stopping me!

THE BROOK

I come from haunts of coot and hern,
I make a sudden sally,
And sparkle out among the fern,
To bicker down a valley,
By thirty hills I hurry down,
Or slip between the ridges,
By twenty thorps, a little town,
And half a hundred bridges.
Till last by Phillip's farm I flow
To join the brimming river,
For men may come and men may go,
But I go on forever.
I chatter over stony ways,
In little sharps and trebles,
I bubble into eddying bays,
I babble on the pebbles.
With many a curve my banks I fret

By many a field and fallow,
And many a fairy foreland set
With willow-weed and mallow.
I charter, chatter, as I flow
To join the brimming river,
For men may come and men may go,
But I go on forever.
I wind about, and in and out,
With here a blossom sailing,
And here and there a lusty trout,
And here and there a grayling.
And here and there a foamy flake
Upon me, as I travel,
With many a silvery water-break
Above the golden gravel,
And draw them all along, and flow
To join the brimming river,
For men may come and men may go,
But I go on forever.
I steal by lawns and grassy plots,
I slide by hazel covers;
I move the sweet forget-me-nots
That grow for happy lovers.
I slip, I slide, I gloom, I glance,
Among my skimming swallows;
I make the netted sunbeam dance
Against my sandy shallows.
I murmur under moon and stars
In brambly wildernesses;
I linger by my shingly bars,
I loiter round my cresses;
And out again I curve and flow
To join the brimming river,
For men may come and men may go,
But I go on forever. (7)

After the first stanza, a crowd began to gather around us. Children stopped playing. Parents stopped rushing about. The sea gulls and galahs were silent. The wind was breathless as were the trees. When Lord Tennyson ended his recital, no one moved. There was silence. Utter and complete silence.

I longed to shout "Encore! Encore!" but knew the clock was ticking. We bid them all adieu, and then continued our journey across the bridge. We stopped to contemplate our reflections and I asked:

Q: Why do you think "In Memoriam" meant so many different things to so many different people?

A: The poem was more the cry of the whole human race than mine. If God allows this strong instinct and universal yearning for another life, surely that is in a measure a presumption of its truth. We cannot give up the mighty hopes that make us men. And for those of us who have loved and lost, let us be consoled with the thought that nothing walks with aimless feet...not one life shall be destroyed, or cast as rubbish to the void, when God hath made the pile complete. We who have been left behind to our sorrows, and whose understanding is that of an infant groping in the night, must never be ashamed to say to ourselves: We need not understand; we love. (8)

Q: You and your wife Emily enjoyed forty years of marriage. Please tell me how you met?

A: It was fourteen years before the publication of "In Memoriam" - when I was still serving my apprenticeship as a poet, when I attended the wedding of my brother Charles. After the ceremony, I met one of the bridesmaids. She was dainty and gracious, and I whispered to her timidly, "Oh, happy bridesmaid, make me a happy bride." When we celebrated our 40th Anniversary, I gave my bride a gift of rosemary and roses. We were as happy on that day, as on the day we were married. (9)

Q: Lord Tennyson, our time is quickly running out, and I would like to ask you one more question. What advice would you like to give to poets in the future?

A: The words of the poet must perform a threefold function. They must supply colour to the inner eye, music to the inner ear and hope to the innermost heart. (10)

I thanked him for his inspiration, and for being my walking companion. I offered him two choices as to how he would like to leave the year 2002. Would he like to change back into his own clothes, or go for a spin in my automobile?

He did not hesitate and, we hopped into the car and before long were cruising along with U2 blasting from the speakers. As we toured around our neighbourhood, Lord Tennyson waved to everyone we passed, laughing impishly when they responded.

I couldn't swear it was true, but I sure thought I heard him singing along with Bono when he reached the chorus of "It's a Beautiful Day, Don't Let It Get Away." (11) Our eyes exchanged glances, as he began to fade. He gave me a gentle wink and disappeared.

Soon I was singing to U2 on my own, heading home. As the garage door opened, I recited the lyric poem written towards the end of Tennyson's life, which was at his request always included at the end of each publication: (12)

CROSSING THE BAR

Sunset and evening star,
And one clear call for me!
And may there be no moaning of the bar,
When I put out to sea,
But such a tide as moving seems asleep,
Too full for sound and foam,
When that which drew from out the boundless deep
Turns again home.
Twilight and evening bell,

And after that the dark!
And may there be no sadness of farewell,
When I embark;
For though from out our bourne of Time and Place
The flood may bear me far,
I hope to see my Pilot face to face
When I have crost the bar. (13)

You cannot go wrong when you read Lord Tennyson's work however these selections receive the highest of recommendations from me:

Idylls of the King
Enoch Arden
The Lotus Eaters
The Princess
The Lady of Shallot
Morte d'Arthur
Ulysses
Becket
The Hesperides
The Day Dream
The Palace of Art
Queen Mary
Harold
The Miller's Daughter
Nothing Will Die
The Ancient Sage
The Two Voices
The Progress of Spring
Merlin and the Gleam
The May Queen
Maud and Other Poems
Lucretius
Ode on the Death of the Duke of Wellington
The Two Voices
The Promise of May

The Cup.

Ta-ta until next time!
Cathy McGough
Your Interviewer of Legendary Writers From Beyond

Chapter Three

EDGAR ALLAN POE AT THE WITCHING HOUR

Welcome everyone. If only you could see what my balcony looks like right now. It is bathed in candlelight! Forty candles to be exact – in celebration of each year of our guest's life.

Yes! Edgar Allan Poe will be joining us this evening – at the witching hour and it is quickly approaching.

Mr. Poe was born on January 19, 1809. While we await his arrival, I shall read aloud the poem he dedicated to his bride Virginia Clemm:

ANNABEL LEE

It was many and many a year ago,
In a kingdom by the sea,
That a maiden there lived whom you may know
By the name of Annabel Lee;
And this maiden she lived with no other thought
Than to love and be loved by me.
I was a child and she was a child,
In this kingdom by the sea,
But we loved with a love that was more than love,

I and my Annabel Lee
With a love that the winged seraphs of Heaven
Coveted her and me.
And this was the reason that, long ago,
In this kingdom by the sea,
A wind blew out of a cloud, chilling
My beautiful Annabel Lee
So that her highborn kinsmen came
And bore her away from me,
To shut her up in a sepulchre
In this kingdom by the sea.
The angels, not half so happy in Heaven,
Went envying her and me
Yes! That was the reason (as all men know,
In this kingdom by the sea)
That the wind came out of the cloud by night,
Chilling and killing my Annabel Lee.
But our love it was stronger by far than the love
Of those who were older than we,
Of many far wiser than we;
And neither the angels the Heaven above,
Nor the demons down under the sea,
Can ever dissever my soul from the soul
Of the beautiful Annabel Lee!
For the moon never beams, without bringing me dreams
Of the beautiful Annabel Lee;
And so, all the night-tide, I lie down by the side
Of my darling – my darling – my life and my bride,
In her sepulchre there by the sea,
In her tomb by the sounding sea. (1)

Sentimental fool that I am - Mr. Poe's words moved my heart up into my throat. I took out my handkerchief and tried to refocus on the questions I had prepared to ask him. Then I looked up and noticed it wasn't Mr. Poe who had come to greet us - it was his treasured wife Virginia Clemm!

Madame Delatour was holding her hand, leading her towards me while Virginia whispered secrets I could not hear into her ear.

Virginia nodded, smiled, curtsied and sat down in the chair opposite to me. Madame Delatour asked if she could speak to me in private for a moment, and we both excused ourselves from Virginia's presence. I pointed to the table filled with cakes and pastries and invited her to partake in them. She reached for a plate, excitedly, as I closed the balcony doors behind me.

"Cathy, Virginia wishes to contact her Edgar. She hasn't seen him since the day she died.

On that fatal winter day, when the side effects from the ruptured blood vessel in her throat became unbearable – Virginia was laid out on a bed with only straw and sheets. Evidently Virginia and Edgar lived in extreme poverty.

Poor thing, all she had was a little kitten Edgar gave her to keep her warm, and Edgar's coat. He held her ice-cold hands in his, and her mother rubbed her feet to keep away the frostbite.

Cathy we cannot let Virginia continue to walk the Heavens all alone. But our decision will have consequences in that Edgar will be with us for less time."

I looked at Virginia. She was only twenty-three years old when she died. Her picturesque beauty. Her dark yet warm eyes. Her strong sense of purpose. Blanchetta was right, we had to reunite the lovers – there was no other choice.

I nodded in the affirmative and Madame Delatour disappeared to summon Mr. Poe.

While we waited, I poured Virginia a strong cup of hot tea and she quickly plopped eight teaspoons full of sugar into her Royal Doulton, and then sighed heavily as she took her first taste. When she went to take a second sip, her hands began to shake wildly, and I hastened to her side to grab a hold of my antique cup and saucer. I wrapped a cloak around her shoulders, turned around and noticed Edgar Allan Poe in the flesh.

He wore a black suit with a knee length jacket, which was buttoned to display an apple red cravat and a snow-white shirt underneath. His eyes were solemn, brooding, and his hair swept across his forehead like a curtain. His nose denoted strength, and his moustached mouth did not form a smile as he looked first at Madame Delatour, then at myself and then finally rested his eyes upon his wife.

Those clear, sad eyes began to tear, full, fuller, and then overflowed as he went to her and clutched her to his bosom. She was like a child still, for he enveloped her with his arms, and she seemed to lose herself there, willingly.

Minutes passed, and then Edgar took a seat. Virginia climbed onto his lap, holding him tightly around the neck. She did not want to let him go for a moment.

Q: You two look very cosy snuggled together. Perhaps you could share a cherished memory?

I knew they were both thinking about the exact same moment when they exchanged glances. Then Edgar began to speak with a gentleness and softness in his voice:

A: It was at the Depot Hotel in the City of New Hope where we had the nicest tea you ever drank, strong and hot – wheat bread and rye bread – cheese – tea cakes (elegant), a great dish of ham and two of cold veal piled up like a mountain in large slices – three dishes of the cakes and everything in the greatest profusion. All I had was ten dollars and we spent most of it on that meal, but so enjoyed it. (2)

Virginia sighed deeply as Edgar stroked her hair and I poured them both a strong cup of tea. Virginia no longer needed my cloak to keep her warm: Edgar was her blanket.

Q: Mr. Poe, I read somewhere that you were paid a paltry sum of $10.00 for publication of "The Raven." Surely, that cannot be true?

A: Please call me Edgar. You are a friend to Virginia and me. But alas, it is true. My greatest work ever, and yet I remained a sad, solitary, hungry writer robed in black, meeting people who knew me, who admired me as a writer yet knowing I was dreaming dreams no mortal ever dreamed before. (3)

Q: Criminal! "The Raven" is still one of the most revered poems of all time. I read somewhere that Charles Dickens inspired you to write it.

A: Charles Dickens was touring the United States and I heard he was coming to Richmond where I lived. I sent him a letter, inviting him to lunch at a downtown Richmond Hotel. Mr. Dickens accepted, and he came to meet me alone. When we sat down to lunch, I noticed that he had been crying. I asked what the matter was, and he said:

I was hoping you wouldn't notice, Mr. Poe, but since you asked, I'll give you an honest answer. I had a personal tragedy in my family before I left England to come to America and I was thinking about it. I have a wife and three children and a pet by the name of "Grip." We loved our pet "Grip" almost as much as we love each other. Before I came away, I took my family on a weekend holiday. We did what we always did with "Grip" was, we locked him in our stable. We left plenty of food and water and thought he would be fine during our absence. But we did not realise there was a large can of paint in the stable, and its lid had fallen off.

Unfortunately, the paint was of a colour that looked just like water. Poor Grip became confused and drank up all the paint by mistake. Imagine our shock, Mr. Poe, when we unlocked the stable door upon our return and there was poor "Grip" -flat on his back, stiff as a board, legs sticking straight up, stone-cold dead.

The phrase "stone-cold dead" echoed in my head. I asked him: What was poor little "Grip?" A cat or a dog?

And Mr. Dickens replied: Oh, no, Mr. Poe, we have no normal pets in our family. Actually "Grip" was a big, lovable black raven. (4)

That night, I went home and revised a poem I had written about a girl named "Lenore." It had been rejected on numerous occasions. I changed the title to "The Raven" and everyone applauded it.

Q: Why do you think "The Raven" captivated readers so?

A: I wanted to write the first adult fairy tale. Critics asked why I didn't begin it with "Once upon a time" then, and I told them: But I did open it that way. In my mind all time is midnight dreary. (5)

Q: Would you please read a little something for us?

A: Listen, listen for in the distance you may hear:

THE BELLS
Hear the sledges with the bells-
Silver bells!
What a world of merriment their melody foretells!
How they tinkle, tinkle, tinkle,
In the icy air of night!
While the stars that over sprinkle
All the heavens, seem to twinkle
With a crystalline delight;
Keeping time, time, time,
In a sort of Runic rhyme,
To the tintinnabulation that so musically wells
From the bells, bells, bells, bells,
Bells, bells, bells-
From the jingling and the tinkling of the bells.
Hear the mellow wedding bells,
Golden bells!
What a world of happiness their harmony foretells!
Through the balmy air of night
How they ring out their delight!

From the molten-golden notes,
And all in tune,
What a liquid ditty floats
To the turtle-dove that listens, while she gloats
On the moon!
Oh, from out the sounding cells,
What a gush of euphony voluminously wells!
How it swells!
How it dwells
On the Future! How it tells
Of the rapture that impels
To the swinging and the ringing
Of the bells, bells, bells,
Of the bells, bells, bells, bells,
Bells, bells, bells-
the rhyming and the chiming of the bells!
Hear the loud alarum bells-
Brazen bells!
What a tale of terror, now, their turbulency tells!
In the startled ear of night
How they scream out their affright!
Too much horrified to speak,
They can only shriek, shriek,
Out of tune,
In a clamorous appealing to the mercy of the fire,
In a mad expostulation with the deaf and frantic fire,
Leaping higher, higher, higher,
With a desperate desire,
And a resolute endeavour,
Now- now to sit or never,
By the side of the pale-faced moon.
Oh, the bells, bells, bells!
What a tale their terror tells
Of Despair!
How they clang, and clash, and roar!

What a horror they outpour
On the bosom of the palpitating air!
Yet the ear it fully knows,
By the twanging,
And the clanging,
How the danger ebbs and flows:
Yet the ear distinctly tells,
In the jangling,
And the wrangling,
How the danger sinks and swells,
By the sinking or the swelling in the anger of the bells-
Of the bells-
Of the bells, bells, bells, bells,
Bells, bells, bells-
In the clamour and the clangour of the bells!
Hear the tolling of the bells-
Iron Bells!
What a world of solemn thought their monody compels!
In the silence of the night,
How we shiver with affright
At the melancholy menace of their tone!
For every sound that floats
From the rust within their throats
Is a groan.
And the people- ah, the people-
They that dwell up in the steeple,
All Alone
And who, tolling, tolling, tolling,
In that muffled monotone,
Feel a glory in so rolling
On the human heart a stone-
They are neither man nor woman-
They are neither brute nor human-
They are Ghouls:
And their king it is who tolls;

And he rolls, rolls, rolls,
Rolls
A paean from the bells!
And his merry bosom swells
With the paean of the bells!
And he dances, and he yells;
Keeping time, time, time,
In a sort of Runic rhyme,
To the paean of the bells-
Of the bells:
Keeping time, time, time,
In a sort of Runic rhyme,
To the throbbing of the bells-
Of the bells, bells, bells-
To the sobbing of the bells;
Keeping time, time, time,
As he knells, knells, knells,
In a happy Runic rhyme,
To the rolling of the bells-
Of the bells, bells, bells:
To the tolling of the bells,
Of the bells, bells, bells, bells-
Bells, bells, bells-
To the moaning and the groaning of the bells. (6)

Q: Thank you Edgar. Please tell me about the extraordinary technique you availed yourself of when studying to be a Journalist?

Edgar smiled, took the hands of his beloved into his, and kissed them and then answered:

A: If I write about taking a journey in a balloon, and want others to believe I did take such a journey, then how can I do that without using things, which existed around me to convince my readers? In some of my books, I have conversations with the dead, and with corpses come to life, these things; these places where my spirit would take me, yet they could only take me so far. After all my dear woman, isn't life a hoax, a fantastic vision plagiarized by some Divine Poet out of the epic nightmare of a diabolical mind? Then why should not I, a human poet, plagiarize the fantastic visions of other human minds? (7)

I quite often referred to foreign books, which, upon investigation, were found never to have existed. I was never handicapped by insufficient education. I loved to show off my acquired knowledge through quotations of passages from languages I knew nothing about. (8)

Q: What advice would you give to writers in the year 2002 and beyond?

A: Learn to work to deadlines. Rely on inspiration. Write quickly. Write in a disordered way. (9)

Q: Our time is ending Mr. Poe and I see your lovely lady has fallen asleep with her arms gently around you. I would like to ask you one final question. Are you an Artist first, or a Poet first?

A: I am first and foremost an artist. I painted the grotesque and the arabesque. I was interested in the beautiful, not the true. The sense of beauty is an immortal instinct deep within the spirit of man. My aim was to evoke beauty through the music of words using whatever literary magical tricks I could employ like novelty, quotation, repetition, unexpected phrases, quaintness's ... sentences and sentiments of sweet sounds that were simply beyond the reach of analysis. No work of art should ever point a moral or embody a truth. That is my opinion. That is how I lived. (10)

Precisely at that moment, hundreds of flying foxes tore across the skies screeching like banshees. We responded to their voices by standing - but when I looked sideways, I noticed both Mr. Poe and Virginia had disappeared into the night.

Perhaps, they flew away on the wings of the bats and are now nestled together in Sydney's Royal Botanical Gardens.

Unable to leave things as they were, I sat down and began to read this poem aloud with the assisted light of the moon:

TO ONE IN PARADISE

Thou wast all that to me, love,
For which my soul did pine;
A green isle in the sea, love,
A fountain and a shrine
All wreathed with fairy fruits and flowers,
And all the flowers were mine.
Ah, dream too bright to last!
Ah, starry Hope, that didst arise
But to be overcast!
"On! On!" – but o'er the Past
(Dim Gulf!) my spirit hovering lies
Must, motionless, aghast.
For, alas! Alas! With me
The light of Life is o'er!
No more – no more – no more –
(Such language holds the solemn sea
To the sands upon the shore)
Shall bloom the thunder-blasted tree,
Or the stricken eagle soar.
And all my days are trances,
And all my nightly dreams
Are where thy gray eye glances,
And where thy footstep gleams –
By that eternal streams. (11)

Then I blew each candle out one by one - 40 wishes floated up to Heaven - Virginia and Edgar together for all of eternity.

Madame Delatour was snoring ever so loudly when I re-entered the house. I was left with a feeling of incompleteness concerning Mr. Poe; yet felt the two spirits re-joining had made it all worthwhile.

I do hope you will feel a strong desire to find out more about the works of Mr. Edgar Allan Poe. Check out these selections and I guarantee you will want more:

The Fall of the House of Usher
The Masque of the Red Death
The Sleeper
A Dream within a Dream
The City and the Sea
Dream-Land
To One in Paradise
The Beautiful Physician
The Haunted Palace
The Conqueror Worm
The Raven
Alone
The Mysterious Star
Epigram for Wall Street
The Murders in the Rue Morgue
The Pit and the Pendulum
Fairyland
The Happiest Days
May Queen Ode
The Power of Words
How to Writer a Blackwood Article
Never Bet the Devil Your Head – A Tale with A Moral
The Purloined Letter
The Oblong Box.

Bye, Bye!
Cathy McGough
Your Interviewer of Legendary Writers From Beyond

Chapter Four

SHELLEY ADMIRES COOKS RIVER

Madame Delatour walked into the living room without our guest of the day: Percy Bysshe Shelley. She was doing her angry walk - while her big purple hoop earrings bounced up and down in synchronicity with her ponytail as it swayed side to side. She wore her summoning purple cape with fluorescent stars and moons she'd embroidered upon it. Her bracelets clinked together as she flung open the patio doors and said:

"What am I to do Cathy? What am I to do? It is Lord Byron. He keeps flirting with me, offering me favours to interview him before Mr. Shelley. He wants to see what two women in the year 2002 are like. He feels he can handle two women of the future much better than Mr. Shelley can, and unfortunately, Mr. Shelley tends to agree. He is blocking Mr. Shelley from crossing over. What shall I do? What shall we do?"

Lord Byron had some cheek! His history with women was well known and interviewing him would be very intriguing. However, interviews are chosen based upon requests made from readers, families and friends. Mr. Byron's interview had been requested, but he was quite a long way down the list.

I persuaded Madame Delatour to advise Lord Byron that we were saving the best for last. Lord Byron's legendary ego would believe it and hopefully things would be back on track with Mr. Shelley.

Percy Bysshe Shelley was born on August 4, 1792 (a fellow Leo!) in Sussex, England. Many years after his death, William Wordsworth is noted as saying of Shelley he was "one of the best artists of us all; in workmanship of style."

Percy formed a friendship with philosopher William Godwin and immediately fell in love with his daughter Mary (even though he was already married with children.) After the tragic suicide of his first wife, he tried to gain custody of his children, but this was denied. Thoroughly disgusted with England's legal system, he departed vowing never to return.

Shelley and Mary soon relocated to Italy where he was to spend the last years of his life. On July 8, 1822, Shelley and his friend were caught in a sudden storm while sailing in a small boat in Lerici, Italy on the coast of the Gulf of Spezia. Their bodies washed up on the shore and in accordance with Italian law, were cremated on the beach in the presence of friends and fellow poets Trelawney, Hunt and Byron. His ashes were taken to Rome and buried near the grave of his dear friend John Keats.

Mr. Shelley was passionate about many things, but poetry was his first love and it is clearly demonstrated in his essay written in response to Thomas Love Peacock's "The Four Ages of Poetry."

In it, Mr. Peacock professed that the art of writing poetry would soon become extinct because men were turning to the great and permanent interests of human society. (1)

Here is an excerpt from Mr. Shelley's rebuttal:

A DEFENCE OF POETRY

Poetry is the record of the best and happiest moments of the happiest and best minds. We are aware of evanescent visitations of thought and feeling, sometimes associated with place or person, sometimes regarding our own mind alone, and always arising unforeseen and departing unbidden, but elevating and delightful beyond all expression; so that even in the desire and the regret they leave, there cannot but be pleasure, participating as it does in the nature of its object. It is as it were the interpenetration of a diviner nature through our own; but its footsteps are like those of a wind over the sea, which the morning calm erases, and whose traces remain only, as on the wrinkled sand which paves it.

These and corresponding conditions of being are experienced principally by those of most delicate sensibility and the most enlarged imagination; and the state of mind produced by them is at war with every base desire. The enthusiasm of virtue, love, patriotism, and friendship is essentially linked with such emotions; and whilst they last, self appears as what it is, an atom to a universe.

Poets are not only subject to these experiences as spirits of the most refined organization, but they can colour all that they combine with the evanescent hues of this ethereal world; a word, a trait in the representation of a scene or a passion will touch the enchanted chord, and reanimate, in those who have ever experienced these emotions, the sleeping, the cold, the buried image of the past. Poetry thus makes immortal all that is best and most beautiful in the world; it arrests the vanishing apparitions which haunt the interlunations of life, and veiling them or in language or in form, sends them forth among mankind, bearing sweet news of kindred joy to those with whom their sisters abide – abide, because there is no portal of expression from the caverns of the spirit which they inhabit into the universe of things.

Poetry redeems from decay the visitations of the divinity of men. (2)

So passionate! So elegantly written! I can't wait to see what Mr. Shelley is like in person.

And for this occasion, I have prepared a plate of Vegemite sandwiches, some Lamingtons and a pot of hot tea is brewing. Nothing like Aussie hospitality!

Now ladies and gentlemen, it looks like we are ready to go as I can see Mr. Shelley being led towards me. Even from a distance his captivating blue eyes and long dark brown curly hair make him seem rather angelic. He is attired in a super fine olive coat with Gilt buttons and a striped Marcela waistcoat. (3) His eyes are somewhat downcast (perhaps he is checking out the carpet), but when he catches a glimpse of the glass doors leading out onto the balcony, he quickly passes his fingers through his hair and walks straight towards the railing saying:

It is just like the great terrace-veranda of my home in Casa Magni, looking out upon the Bay of Spezia where there were also sea-views and landscapes of unparalleled loveliness. (4) Are there boats nearby? May I sail today?

Our eyes locked for the first time, and close up he was like a child you could not refuse. However, our time was limited, and I needed to let him know what he was looking at, i.e., Cooks River, not the ocean - and to explain where we were in Australia. When I confirmed there was not time to sail, he pouted ever so slightly until he was distracted by the unfamiliar sounds of kookaburras and magpies. In the distance the gum trees and jacarandas danced in the breeze as I poured Mr. Shelley a cuppa.

As we sat down, Mr. Shelley stared into my eyes. When we made contact, he looked away.

I went back to my notes and soon caught his eyes locked onto mine once again. I wasn't certain what he was looking at. In fact, I wasn't certain about anything at that moment. I felt a hot blush rising upon my cheek.

The intensity of his gaze continued.

Since I have been interviewing – I have developed a sense of confidence when in the presence of these masters. I generally feel relaxed, although somewhat in awe.

However, Mr. Shelley's constant gazing and then looking away was making me fidgety.

I attempted to regain composure by shuffling through some papers when he, ever the sensitive soul - spotted my reddish hue.

My apologies, dear lady. I do not mean to make you feel self-conscious. It is your eyes. Those piercing hazel eyes (5) of yours. You see, I have seen them before in the fair and shapely head of my wife Mary.

For a moment I was speechless. However, I managed to peep out a mousey thank you. For a few seconds we looked out into the distance, until I was fully in control and then the interview began.

Q: Please tell me about a special moment you shared with Mary.

A: I enjoyed the moments when she followed me to the place where I moored my boat. There, she would lie with her head upon my knee and close her tired eyes. I would caress her golden head. We would breathe in the sea air and let the soft gentle breeze lull us gently. It was as if we were in a world all our own. (6)

Q: Oh, how romantic! This is rather a strange change of topic, but I read somewhere that you and Mary were vegetarian? In fact, today, it is a very popular lifestyle.

A: I am afraid being vegetarian was by necessity, not choice. If we were lucky enough to be able to buy some meat both Mary and I used to make certain the children had it. I lived mostly on bread, carrying a chunk of it in my pocket wherever I went lest I should forget to eat entirely. Poetry gave me sustenance. (7)

Q: What did you miss the most during your voluntary exile from England?

A: Homesickness caught me off guard now and again, and my remedy for this was reading the works of the Lake Poets and in particular the words of William Wordsworth. Our Poets and our Philosophers, our mountains and our lakes, the rural lanes and fields which are ours so especially, are ties which unless I become utterly senseless can never be broken asunder. These and the memory of them if I never shall return, these and the affections of the mind with which having once been united they are inseparably united, even if I should permanently return to it no more. (8)

It is also extremely difficult to find a good cup of tea when one is abroad.

Q: How is it you came to be known as "Mad Shelley?" (9)

A: I often got up to experiments with chemicals and magic. The other children used to tease me relentlessly and follow me about and even go on what they called "Shelley Hunts." There was a day though, when things really escalated. It was during my stay at Eton. I drew a circle and stood in the centre of it. The other students gathered around me as I poured alcohol into a little plate and set it on fire. I watched it take on its bluish flame and then began reciting things such as: "Demons come out and join us!" A teacher noticed me and shouted, asking what I was doing. I told him I was trying to raise the devil. (10)

Q: Is it true you used your siblings in your experiments?

A: My sister Hellen's Journal best describes my antics. Remember I was but eleven years of age:

When my brother commenced his studies in chemistry, and practised electricity upon us, I confess my pleasure in it was entirely negatived by terror at its effects. Whenever he came to me with his piece of folded brown packing paper under his arm and a bit of wire and a bottle, my heart would sink with fear at his approach; but shame kept me silent, and, with as many others as he could collect, we were placed hand-in-hand round the nursery table to be electrified. (11)

Q: And speaking of things electric - what are your thoughts on love?

A: I always expected more of love, demanded more of love than it was able to give in return. Consequently, love always disappointed me. One is always in love with something or other; the error consists in seeking in the image the likeness of what is eternal. (12)

Q: Who influenced your work the most?

A: Plato without dispute. Plato was essentially a poet. The truth and splendour of his imagery and the melody of his language is the most intense that it is possible to conceive. He rejected the harmony in thoughts divested of shape and action, and he forbore to invent any regular pauses of his style. (13) I translated his "Ion" - part of "Phased" and several epigrams. I wrote this for him:

MORNING AND EVENING STAR

THOU art the morning star among the living,
Ere thy fair light had fled;
Now, having died, thou art as Hesperus, giving
New splendour to the dead. (14)

Yet I cannot fail to remember Dante. Dante was the first awakener of entranced Europe; he created a language, in itself music and persuasion, out of chaos of inharmonious barbarisms. He was the congregator of those great spirits who presided over the resurrection of learning, the Lucifer of that starry flock which in the thirteenth century shone forth from republican Italy, as from a heaven, into the darkness of the benighted world. His very words are instinct with spirit; each is as a spark, a burning atom of inextinguishable thought; and many yet lie covered in the ashes of their birth and pregnant with a lightning that has yet found no conductor. (15)

Q: Define Poet?

A: Poets, according to the circumstances of the age and nation in which they appeared, were called, in the earlier epochs of the world, legislators, or prophets: a poet essentially comprises and unites both these characters. For he not only beholds intensely the present as it is and discovers those laws according to which present things ought to be ordered, but he beholds the future in the present, and his thoughts are the germs of the flower of the fruit of latest time. Not that I assert poets to be the prophets in the gross sense of the word. A poet participates in the eternal, the infinite, and the one. (16)

Q: Does a poet require a formal education or simply the education of life?

A: There is an education peculiarly fitted for a Poet, without which genius and sensibility can hardly fill the circle of their capacities... The circumstances of my accidental education have been favourable to this ambition. I have been familiar from boyhood with mountains and lakes and the sea, and the solitude of forests: Danger, which sports upon the brink of precipices, has been my playmate. I have trodden the glaciers of the Alps and lived under the eye of Mont Blanc. I have been a wanderer among distant fields. I have sailed down mighty rivers, and seen the sun rise and set, and the stars come forth, whilst I have sailed night and day down a rapid stream among mountains. I have seen populous cities, and have watched the passions, which rise and spread, and sink and change, amongst assembled multitudes of men.

I have seen the theatre of the more visible ravages of tyranny and war; cities and villages reduced to scattered groups of black and roofless houses, and the naked inhabitants sitting famished upon their desolate thresholds.

I have conversed with living men of genius. The poetry of ancient Greece and Rome, and modern Italy, and our own country, has been to me, like eternal nature, a passion and an enjoyment. Such are the sources from which the materials for the imagery of my Poems have been drawn. I have considered Poetry in its most comprehensive sense; and have read the Poets and the Historians and the Metaphysicians whose writings have been accessible to me, and have looked upon the beautiful and majestic scenery of the earth, as common sources of those elements which it is the province of the Poet to embody and combine... How far I shall be found to possess the more essential attribute of Poetry, the power of awakening in the other sensations like those which animate my own bosom, is that which, to speak sincerely, I do not know. (17)

Q: What is your opinion of fellow poet and friend Lord Byron?

A: Lord Byron was an exceedingly interesting person, and as such it is to be regretted that he was a slave to the vilest and most vulgar prejudices, and as mad as the winds! (18)

Q: I shall certainly keep that in mind when I interview him! You did quite a lot of travelling. If you had to choose one site as your favourite, which would you choose?

A: The Colosseum: It had been changed by time into the image of an amphitheatre of rocky hills overgrown by the wild olive, the myrtle and the fig tree, and threaded by little paths which wind among its ruined stairs and immeasurable galleries; the copse-wood overshadows you as you wander through its labyrinths and the wild weeds of the climate of flowers bloom under your feet...I could scarcely believe that when encrusted with Dorian marble and ornamented by columns of Egyptian granite its effect could have been so sublime and impressive. (19)

Q: What would you like to convey to Poets in the year 2002?

A: We have more moral, political, and historical wisdom than we know how to reduce into practise; we have more scientific and economic knowledge than can be accommodated to the just distribution of the produce, which it multiplies.

The poetry in these systems of thought is concealed by the accumulation of facts and calculating processes...We want the creative faculty to imagine that which we know; we want the generous impulse to act that which we imagine; we want the poetry of life; our calculations have outrun our conception...The cultivation of those sciences which have enlarged the limits of the empire of man over the external world has far want of the poetical faculty proportionally circumscribed those of the internal world; and man, having enslaved the elements, remains himself a slave. (20)

Q: Percy before you go – could you please read "The Cloud." It is my favourite.

A: By special request then, just for you dearest lady:

THE CLOUD

I bring fresh showers for the thirsting flowers,
From the seas and the streams;
I bear light shade for the leaves when laid
In their noonday dreams.
From my wings are shaken the dews that waken
The sweet buds every one,
When rocked to rest on their mother's breast,
As she dances about the sun.
I wield the flail of the lashing hail,
And whiten the green plains under,
And then again I dissolve it in rain,
And laugh as I pass in thunder.
I sift the snow on the mountains below,
And their great pines groan aghast;
And all the night 'tis my pillow white,
While I sleep in the arms of the blast.
Sublime on the towers of my skiey bowers,
Lightning my pilot sits;
In a cavern under is fettered the thunder,
It struggles and howls at fits;

Over earth and ocean, with gentle motion,
This pilot is guiding me,
Lured by the love of the genii that move
In the depths of the purple sea;
Over the rills, and the crags, and the hills,
Over the lakes and the plains,
Wherever he dream, under mountain or stream,
The Spirit he loves remains;
And I all the while bask in Heaven's blue smile,
Whilst he is dissolving in rains.
The sanguine Sunrise, with his meteor eyes,
And his burning plumes outspread,
Leaps on the back of my sailing rack,
When the morning star shines dead;
As on the jag of a mountain crag,
Which an earthquake rocks and swings,
An eagle alit one moment may sit
In the light of its golden wings.
And when Sunset may breathe, from the lit sea beneath,
Its ardours of rest and of love,
And the crimson pall of eve may fall
From the depth of Heavens above,
With wings unfolded I rest, on mine aery nest,
As still as a brooding dove.
That orbed maiden with white fire laden,
Whom mortals call the Moon
Glides glimmering o'er my fleece-like-floor,
By the midnight breezes strewn;
And wherever the beat of her unseen feet,
Which only the angels hear,
May have broken the woof of my tent's thin roof,
The stars peep behind her and peer;
And I laugh to see them whirl and flee,
Like a swarm of golden bees,
When I widen the rent in my wind-built tent,

Till the calm rivers, lakes, and seas,
Like strips of the sky fallen through me on high,
Are each paved with the moon and these.
I bind the Sun's throne with a burning zone,
And the Moon's with a girdle of pearl;
The volcanoes are dim, and the stars reel and swim,
When the whirlwinds my banner unfurl.
From cape to cape, with a bridge-like shape,
Over a torrent sea,
Sunbeam-proof, I hang like a roof, -
The mountains its columns be.
The triumphal arch through which I march
With hurricane, fire and snow,
When the Powers of the air are chained to my chair,
Is the million-coloured bow;
The sphere-fire above its soft colours wove,
While the moist Earth was laughing below.

He stopped abruptly and noticed that I had continued speaking the words, cleared his throat, smiled and continued...

I am the daughter of Earth and Water,
And the nursling of the Sky;
I pass through the pores of the ocean and shores,
I change, but I cannot die.
For after the rain when with never a stain
The pavilion of Heaven is bare,
And the winds and the sunbeams with their convex gleams
Build up the blue dome of air,
I silently laugh at my own cenotaph,
And out of the caverns of rain,
Like a child from the womb, like a ghost from the tomb,
I arise and unbuild it again. (21)

While he was reading, he began to fade in and out, like a bad transmission and by the time he finished the final line, he had disappeared entirely.

I hope you have caught the Shelley bug and encourage you to seek out his works.

I recommend the following:

Prometheus Unbound
The Cloud
Adonais
Queen Mab
The Mask of Anarchy
To a Skylark
Ode to the West Wind
To the Moon
A Lament
Laon and Cyntha
Love's Philosophy
Hymn to the Spirit of Nature
The Poet's Dream
Lines to an Indian Air
The Cenci
To Night
I Fear Thy Kisses
The Flight of Love
Ozymandias of Egypt
To a Lady with a Guitar
The Invitation
The Recollection
The Spirit of Solitude
Alastor
Rosalind and Helen
A Dream of the Unknown
Music, When Soft Voices Die
The Indian Serenade
Triumph of Life
A Defence of Poetry.

Join me next week when Madame Delatour will bring another guest to my humble abode. For now, she requires a large Scotch on the rocks because Lord Byron is still hanging around like a bad penny trying to convince us to interview him next. Sorry, no can do Lord Byron – the public decides!

Ta, ta!

Cathy McGough
Your Interviewer of Legendary Writers From Beyond

Chapter Five

WILKIE COLLINS WEAVES A TALE

Have you discovered the works of Wilkie Collins? If you haven't stumbled upon some of his novels at your local bookstore then you are truly missing out!

Wilkie Collins was born on January 8, in 1824 in New Cavendish Street, London, England. Mr. Collins left his readers an enormous legacy consisting of twenty-five novels, over fifty short stories, nearly fifteen plays and over one hundred non-fiction pieces of work. His novels "The Moonstone" and "The Woman in White" are two classics. Wilkie Collins was educated in the field of law, which served him well when he wrote his melodramatic but meticulous thrillers.

Madame Delatour notified me that Mr. Collins was on his way out – and within seconds I noticed him walking towards me. He looked around, inquisitive as a cat while I introduced myself and thanked him for coming to meet me.

He sat down briefly, and then suddenly bolted upright – waving his hands emphatically and pointing towards the sky: Wilkie Collins had discovered the art of skywriting.

He watched the jet stream, like a child in anticipation of its message. For a moment, I thought he had stopped breathing entirely; he was so overwhelmed by the words being written.

The jet stream stopped, and the word "Nokia" revealed itself to my guest. He looked at me, then at the message and read it aloud over and over again, like someone trying to decipher a secret code.

I explained it's meaning, and Mr. Collins was very disappointed. He commented that the world had stooped to an all-time low, in allowing pollution of the Heavens for advertising.

I hadn't thought of skywriting in quite that way before...soon enough the jet stream faded away and our interview began.

Q: When did you first meet Charles Dickens?

A: Charles and I met on March 12, 1851. I had accepted the part of Smart the Valet in the amateur production of Bulwer-Lytton's play "Not So Bad as We Seem." Charles was twelve years older than I was, and he was already an established author and public figure. Even so, we became lifelong friends. I dedicated my book "Hide and Seek" to him in 1854, "To Charles Dickens this story is inscribed as a token of admiration and affection, by his friend, the author."

I was employed in "Household Words" for five years, and later "All The Year Round." We also collaborated on Christmas issues for both publications including "No Thoroughfare." (1)

Q: Have you always loved telling stories?

A: As a young boy, at second school in Highbury where I was a boarder, I was regularly bullied by the head boy.

"You will go to sleep, Collins," he said, "When you have told me a story."

It was this brute who first awakened in me, his poor victim, a power of which but for him I might never have been aware...When I left school, I continued storytelling for my own pleasure. (2)

Q: You tried to show life as it was although the public oftentimes wanted to make like ostriches.

A: We have become so shamelessly familiar with violence and outrage, that we recognise them as a necessary ingredient in our social system, and class our savages as a representative part of our population under the newly invented name of "roughs." Public attention has been directed by hundreds of other writers to the dirty Rough in fustian. If I had confined myself within those limits, I would have carried all my readers with me. But I am bold enough to direct attention to the washed Rough in broadcloth – and I must stand on my defence with readers who have not noticed this variety, or who, having noticed, prefer to ignore it.

Is no protest needed, in the interests of civilization, against a revival of barbarism among us, which asserts itself to be a revival of manly virtue, and finds human stupidity actually dense enough to admit the claim? (3)

Q: I'm sorry to inform you that things haven't changed very much today. You must wonder if they ever will. Perhaps this might be a good time to ask you to read something from one of your books?

A: "Basil" was the second work of fiction, which I produced. On its appearance, it was condemned off-hand by a certain class of readers, as an outrage on their sense of propriety. I knew that "Basil" had nothing to fear from pure-minded readers; and I left those pages to stand or fall on such merits as they possessed. Slowly and surely, my story forced its way through all adverse criticism, to a place in the public favour, which I hope it has never lost since.

This is taken from Part I, Chapter II of:

BASIL

I might attempt, in this place, to sketch my own character as it was at that time. But what man can say – I will sound the depth of my own vices, and measure the height of my own virtues; and be as good as his word? We can neither know nor judge ourselves; others may judge but cannot know us; God alone judges and knows too. Let my character appear – as far as any human character can appear in its integrity, in this world – in my actions, when I describe the one eventful passage in my life, which forms the basis for this narrative. In the meantime, it is first necessary that I should say more about the members of my family. Two of them at least, will be found important to the progress of events in these pages. I make no attempt to judge their characters; I only describe them – whether rightly or wrongly, I know not – as they appeared to me. (4)

Q: It has been said that you were a "compulsive reviser." Is that a fair statement?

A: Fair? What is fair? I revised. For someone to call me a "compulsive reviser" they must have seen manuscripts and proofs of my novels. I did go over them in detail before publication, altering, adding, and deleting until the page became a virtually unreadable palimpsest. Whenever a new edition of a novel was called for, I took the opportunity to revise it again. Usually the changes I made were minor changes of punctuation and sentence structure. The exception was "Hide and Seek" where the changes were far more extensive. It was dedicated to my dear friend Charles Dickens therefore I needed to make it as perfect as it could be. In the preface to the 1861 edition I wrote: I have abridged, and in many cases omitted, several passages...which made larger demands upon the reader's patience than I should now think it is desirable to venture on. (5)

Q: Some critics allege "Hide and Seek" was autobiographical due to the appearance of your family pet "Snooks."

A: Alas, the only part of "Hide and Seek" that was autobiographical was my dear kitten "Snooks" I recall writing to my mother in 1844, complaining of the housemaid's behaviour towards it:

I lectured her the other day upon inhumanity. In her zeal for Science, or for her kitchen (I don't know which) she attempted to reintroduce by the kitten's nose that which the innocent animal had just previously expelled as worthless from an opposite and inferior portion of its body. Charles (my brother) tried rage upon the subject with the cook. I tried philosophy with the housemaid. He failed. I succeeded – Purified was the nose of "Snooks." (6)

Q: Would you mind explaining your ideas on the family of fiction?

A: Believing that the Novel and the Play are twin-sisters in the family of Fiction; that the one is a drama narrated, as the other is a drama acted; and that all the strong and deep emotions which the Play-writer is privileged to excite, the Novel-writer is privileged to excite also, I have not thought it either politic or necessary, while adhering to realities, to adhere to every-day realities only. In other words, I have not stooped so low as to assure myself of the reader's belief in the probability of my story, but never once calling on him for the exercise of his faith. Those extraordinary accidents and events which happen to few men seemed to me to be as legitimate materials for fiction to work with – when there was a good object in using them – as the ordinary accidents and events which may, and do, happen to us all. By appealing to genuine sources of interest within the reader's own experience, I could certainly gain his attention to begin with; but it would be only by appealing to other sources (as genuine in their way) beyond his own experience, that I could hope to fix his interest and excite his suspense, to occupy his deeper feelings, or to stir his nobler thoughts. (7)

Q: Is it the Novelist's role to present realism to its readers?

A: To those persons who dissent from the broad principles here adverted to; who deny that it is the novelist's vocation to do more than merely amuse them; who shrink from all honest and serious reference in books, to subjects they think of in private and talk of in public everywhere; who see covert implications where nothing is implied and improper allusions where nothing improper is alluded to; whose innocence is in the word, and not in the thought; whose morality stops at the tongue, and never gets on to the heart – to those persons, I should consider it a loss of time, and worse, to offer any further explanation of my motives, than the sufficient explanation which I have given already. I do not address myself to them in this interview and shall never think of addressing myself to them in any other. (8)

Q: In "No Name" I believe you tried something no Novelist had ever attempted before.

A: The only secret contained in the book was revealed midway in the first volume. From that point, all the main events of the story were purposely foreshadowed before they took place – my design being to rouse the reader's interest in following the train of circumstances by which those foreseen events were brought about. In trying this new ground, I was not turning my back in doubt on the ground, which I had passed over already. My one object in following a new course was to enlarge the range of my studies in the art of writing fiction, and to vary the form in which I made my appeal to the reader, as attractively as I could. (9)

NO NAME

The First Scene

The hands on the hall-clock pointed to half-past six in the morning. The house was a country residence in West Somerset Shire called Combe-Raven. The day was the fourth of March, and the year was 1846.

No sounds but the steady ticking of the clock, and the lumpish snoring of a large dog stretched on a mat outside the dining room door, disturbed the mysterious morning stillness of hall and staircase. Who were the sleepers hidden in the upper regions? Let the house reveal its own secrets; and, one by one, as they descend the stairs from their beds, let the sleepers disclose themselves.

As the clock pointed to a quarter to seven, the dog woke and shook himself. After waiting in vain for the footman, who was accustomed to let him out, the animal wandered restlessly from one closed door to another on the ground-floor; and returning to his mat in great perplexity, appealed to the sleeping family, with a long and melancholy howl.

Before the last notes of the dog's remonstrance had died away, the oaken stairs in the higher regions of the house creaked under slowly descending footsteps. In a minute more the first of the female servants made her appearance, with a dingy woollen shawl over her shoulders – for the March morning was bleak; and rheumatism and the cook were old acquaintances.

Receiving the dog's first cordial advances with the worst possible grace, the cook slowly opened the hall door and let the animal out. It was a wild morning. Over a spacious lawn, and behind a black plantation of firs, the rising sun rent its way upward through piles of ragged grey cloud; heavy drops of rain fell few and far between; the March wind shuddered round the corners of the house, and the wet trees swayed wearily. (10)

Q: I'm certain our readers are intrigued and will be running out to their local bookstore to find out what happens. For those who have not read "No Name" would you mind explaining the premise of the book?

A: The main purpose of the story, is to appeal to the reader's main interest in a subject which has been the theme of some of the greatest writers, living and dead – but which has never been, and can never be, exhausted, because it is a subject eternally interesting to all mankind. It is one more book depicting the struggle of a human creature, under those opposing influences of Good and Evil, which we all have felt, which we all have known. (11)

Q: "No Name" tells how a brutal twist of fate alters the existence of two sisters. Novels written about such serious subject matter rarely have humour in them.

A: I sought to impart that relief to the more serious passages in the book, not only because I believed myself to be justified in doing so by the laws of Art – but because experience taught me that there is no such moral phenomenon as unmixed tragedy to be found in the world around us. Look where we may, the dark threads and the light cross each other perpetually in the texture of human life. (12)

Q: No writer has come close to you Mr. Collins, in enticing readers into the world you have created. A perfect example which immediately comes to mind is your short story: "Mr. Policeman and the Cook" – would you mind reading the first few paragraphs of the story?

A: If time would permit me to, I would read it, in its entirety. However, due to time constraints these few paragraphs must suffice:

MR. POLICEMAN AND THE COOK

A First Word For Myself

Before the Doctor left me one evening, I asked him how much longer I was likely to live. He answered: "It's not easy to say; you may die before I can get back to you in the morning, or you may live to the end of the month."

I was alive enough on the next morning to think of the needs of my soul, and (being a member of the Roman Catholic Church) to send for the priest.

The history of my sins, related in confession, included blameworthy neglect of a duty, which I owed to the laws of my country. In the priest's opinion – and I agreed with him – I was bound to make public acknowledgement of my fault, as an act of penance becoming to a Catholic Englishman. We concluded, thereupon, to try a division of labour. I related the circumstances, while his reverence took the pen, and put the matter into shape.

Here follows what came of it: - (13)

Once again, my dear readers in order for you to find out what happens you will have to read the book!

Q: Do you have any advice to impart to writers in the future?

A: Make'em laugh, make'em cry, make'em wait. (14)

When Mr. Collins finished speaking, he faded in and out for a second, and then disappeared. His final words echoed in my mind, as I rolled them over and over upon my tongue, "Make'em laugh, make'em cry, make'em wait." Words to live by!

Here are some of Mr. Collins' works you should definitely put on your MUST-READ list:

Armadale
The Woman In White
No Name
The Moonstone
Basil: A Story of Modern Life
My Lady's Money
Legacy of Cain
Hide and Seek
Man and Wife
Little Novels
The Dead Secret
The Queen of Hearts
Gabriel's Marriage
Rambles Beyond Railways
No Thoroughfare
Poor Miss Finch

The Frozen Deep and Other Stories
The Law and the Lady
The Fallen Leaves
The Evil Genius
The Black Robe
The Haunted Hotel
Blind Love
The Lazy Tour of Two Idle Apprentices.

For now, CHEERIO!
Cathy McGough
Your Interviewer of Legendary Writers From Beyond

Chapter Six

NEW YEAR'S EVE WITH ROBBIE BURNS

Welcome one and all to the Tam O'Shanter Pub. Have a wee dram while we await the arrival of our honoured guest: Mr. Robbie Burns!

In the meantime, let me tell you a little bit about him. Robbie Burns was born on January 25th (now celebrated as Robbie Burns Day) in a furious blizzard in Ayrshire, Scotland, in 1759. His father was a farmer, and Robbie tried everything possible to follow in his footsteps, but his heart was not in it. His heart wanted to sing, and to soar across the Scottish Highlands, which he loved so well.

Alas, Robbie was diagnosed with the symptoms of a rheumatic heart, thus he was not long for this world. He died in 1796, leaving an amazing repertoire.

To know Robbie Burns, his heart and mind more fully, you need to read everything he wrote. For the more you read, the more his spirit will be revealed to you.

Madame Delatour has just given me the nod that she will be going into a secluded area in the back of the pub to contact Mr. Burns, so he should be with us in just a few moments.

Meanwhile, I have asked the ever-growing crowd to keep it down, so they don't intimidate Mr. Burns. Once he is comfortable in his new surroundings, I will ask his permission to allow this gang of rowdies to join us. I only hope they can contain their excitement long enough! After all, this Pub was named for Robbie Burns and everyone who gathers here, gathers in his name.

Let us begin, with a poem Robbie penned during a very dark time when he contemplated leaving Scotland forever:

THE LAMENT

O'er the mist-shrouded cliffs of their lone mountain straying,
Where the wild winds of winter incessantly rave,
What woes wring my heart while intently surveying
The storm's gloomy path on the breast of the wave!
Ye foam-crested billows, allow me to wail,
Ere ye toss me afar from my loved native shore;
Where the flower which bloomed sweetest in Coila's green vale,
The pride of my bosom, my Mary's no more!
No more by the banks of the streamlet we'll wander,
And smile at the moon's rimpled face in the wave;
No more shall my arms cling with fondness around her,
For the dewdrops of morning fall cold on her grave.
No more shall the soft thrill of love warm my breast;
I haste with the storm to a far-distant shore;
Where, unknown, unlamented, my ashes shall rest,
And joy shall revisit my bosom no more. (1)

Madame Delatour caught my attention confirming that our visitor had arrived.

I grabbed a bottle of Glenfiddich Malt Scotch Whiskey, several glasses, mixed nuts and pretzels then made my way into the back room. The owner of the Pub offered to have his rather buxom barmaid bring it in on a tray, but quite frankly I didn't want or need the competition for Mr. Burns' attention.

The room was buzzing in anticipation of The Bard's arrival. I attempted to capture their attention without luck. Finally, I had to resort to a full assault upon their ears with a loud blast from the Captain's Whistle, which I sported around my neck.

Thank goodness the clamour ended instantly – so I had the opportunity to ask them to keep it down. After all we didn't want to scare off Mr. Burns.

His name brought on another tumultuous roar, which I silenced by offering to buy the next round of drinks and then high tailing it out of there. I looked over my shoulder at the chaos I'd created and hoped the barman would forgive me.

When I peered through the porthole, which looked in upon the backroom and saw Robbie Burns standing there I gasped.

He was drop dead gorgeous and sported a devastating dimple on his chin (which reminded me of Cary Grant's.) He stood close to 6 ft. tall, with charcoal black hair, and even from a distance I could see that he had mysterious dark eyes. His eyes I would easily classify as bedroom eyes - and knew instantly why he had such a reputation with the ladies.

Madame Delatour was seated, looking up at him with her eyelids all a flutter when I entered the room and introduced myself. My knees went weak, as he took the heavy tray from my hands and placed it upon the table. Then he poured a glass of Scotch for each of us and smiled as his eyes roamed around the room.

Anxious to begin the interview, I gave Madame Delatour the eye - from her to the door, then back to her again - but she didn't seem to get the hint.

Since time was ticking away, I had no choice – and gently kicked her under the table. That seemed to do the trick.

Madame Delatour exited, with the guise of offering us some privacy – then rolled her eyes at me as she bumped into the swinging doors.

Although she made an excuse to leave us to our interview, I was sure she was off to the ladies to give her face a quick splash of cold water. Mr. Burns had made quite an impression upon Madame Delatour.

In a few seconds, I became less star struck, and welcomed Mr. Burns to the Tam o'Shanter Pub in Sydney, Australia.

Just in case Blanchetta hadn't informed him, I explained that we were just about to ring in the year 2003. Then our interview began.

Q: Who inspired you as a child?

A: In my infant and boyish days I owe much to an old woman named Betty Davidson who was taken in by our family. Betty was remarkable for her ignorance, credulity and superstition. She had, I suppose, the largest collection in the country of tales and songs concerning devils, ghosts, fairies, brownies, witches, warlocks, spunkies, kelpies, elf-candles, dead-lights, wraiths, apparitions, cantraips, giants, enchanted towers, dragons and other trumpery. This cultivated the latent seeds of poetry, but had so strong an effect on my imagination that to this hour, in my nocturnal rambles, I sometimes keep a sharp lookout in suspicious places; and though nobody can be more sceptical than I am in such matters, yet it often takes an effort of philosophy to shake off these idle terrors. (2)

Q: Were your talents for writing recognized then?

A: When I was a child, I was a good deal noted for retentive memory, a stubborn, sturdy something in my disposition and an enthusiastic idiot piety. I say idiot piety, because I was then but a child. Though it cost the schoolmaster some thrashings, I made an excellent English scholar, and by the time I was ten or eleven years of age I was a critic in substantives, verbs and particles. (3)

Q: Which books if any captured your imagination as a boy?

A: The first two books I ever read in private, and which gave me more pleasure than any two books I ever read since, were "The Life of Hannibal" and "The History of Sir William Wallace."

Hannibal gave my young ideas such a turn, that I used to strut in raptures up and down after the recruiting drum and bagpipe, and wish myself tall enough to be a soldier; while the story of Wallace poured a Scottish prejudice into my veins which will always be in my heart and my mind. (4)

Q: Why did you first start writing poetry?

A: To amuse myself with the little creations of my own fancy, amid the toil and fatigue of a laborious life; to transcribe the various feelings – the loves, the griefs, the hopes, the fears – in my own breast; to find some kind of counterpoise to the struggles of a world, always an alien scene, a task uncouth to the poetical mind – these were my motives for courting the Muses, and in these I found Poetry to be its own reward. (5)

Q: You never considered publishing?

A: None of my works were composed with a view to the press. Though a rhymer from my earliest years, at least from the earliest impulse of the softer passions, it was not till very late that the applause, perhaps the partiality, of friendship, awakened my vanity so far as to make me think anything of my works worth showing. (6)

Q: Once you saw your works in print, surely you knew that you were a talented Poet?

A: I appeared in the public with fear and trembling. I, an obscure, nameless Bard, shrunk aghast at the thought of being branded as – an impertinent blockhead, obtruding my nonsense on the world; and, because I could make shift to jingle a few doggerel Scottish rhymes together, looked upon myself as a Poet, of no smail consequence, forsooth! (7)

Q: How did you come to write your first song?

A: The Poetic Genius of my Country found me, at the Plough; and threw her inspiring mantle over me. She bade me sing the loves, the joys, the rural scenes, and rural pleasures of my native soil, in my native tongue; I turned my wild, artless notes as she inspired. She whispered to me to come to this ancient Metropolis of Caledonia and lay my Songs under her honoured protection: I then obeyed her dictates. As farmers, we had a country custom of coupling a man and a woman together as partners in the labours of harvest. In my fifteenth autumn my partner was a bewitching creature, a year younger than myself.

My scarcity of English denies me the power of doing her justice I that language; but you know the Scottish idiom – she was a bonnie, sweet, sonsie lass. In short, she, altogether unwittingly to herself, initiated me in that delicious passion, which, in spite of acid disappointment, gin-horse prudence, and bookworm philosophy, I hold to be the first of human joys, our dearest blessing! Among her other love-inspiring qualities, she sang sweetly; and it was her favourite reel to which I attempted giving an embodied vehicle in rhyme.

When my girl sang a song, which was said to be composed by a small country laird's son, I saw no reason why I might not rhyme as well as he. (8)

Madame Delatour was back – spying on us through the port-hole. Fortunately, Mr. Burns could not see her being a cheeky little monkey. She tried blowing kisses in his direction – but she couldn't will him to turn around. Bothered and bewildered - she gave up!

Q: Her name was Mary Campbell: Your first love. Please tell me about her.

A: Mary consented to be my wife. We were to be separated and met in secret on the second Sunday in May, in a lonely spot on the banks of the Ayr. We stood on each side of a small purling brook. We dipped our hands in the limpid stream, and holding a Bible between us, pronounced our vows to each other. We then exchanged Bibles. In the one I gave to Mary, I had written "And ye shall not swear by my name falsely. I am the Lord. Thou shalt not forswear thyself but shall perform unto the Lord thine oaths." (9)

Q: Robbie, you will be very pleased to learn that very Bible has been preserved and placed in Mary's monument. (10)

Robbie took out his handkerchief, and wiped the tears from his eyes as he began reciting:

TO MARY IN HEAVEN

THOU lingering star, with lessening ray,
That love'st to greet the early morn,
Again thou sher'st in the day
My Mary from my soul was torn. (11)

I poured Robbie another drink, which he tossed back and pushed his glass towards me for another. I marvelled at how love can exist in time and space and held back a very strong urge to take him into my arms and comfort him. Instead I kept my mind focussed and went ahead with the next question.

Q: What advice would you give to writers in 2003 and beyond?

A: The best advice I can give you is to know yourself. Make of yourself a constant study. Weigh yourself along, balance yourself with others. Watch every means of information, to see how much ground you occupy as a person and as a poet. Study assiduously nature's design and formation – to see where the lights and shades in your character are intended. (12)

All at once bagpipes began to sound. Just a few minutes to go until midnight!

Q: Would you mind singing a few songs to help us bring in the New Year? An audience is waiting outside to meet you. May I ask them to join us?

A: The more the merrier I always say.

Robbie started singing as the pipers paraded into the room and joined him:

A RED, RED, ROSE

O, My luve's like a red, red rose,
That's newly sprung in June:
O, my luve's like the melodie
That's sweetly played in tune.
As fair art thou, my bonnie lass,
So deep in luve am I;
And I will luve thee still my dear,
Till a' the seas gang dry.
Till a' the seas gang dry, my dear,
And the rocks melt wi' the sun:
I will luve thee still, my dear,
While the sands o' life shall run.
And far thee weel, my only luve!
And fare thee weel a while!
And I will come again, my luve,
Though it were ten thousand mile. (13)

We moved into a tumultuous applause, while Robbie prepared himself for an encore. No way he was getting out of there without doing more than one tune!

MY HEART'S IN THE HIGHLANDS

My heart's in the Highlands, my heart is not here;
My heart's in the highlands, a-chasing the deer;
Chasing the wild deer, and following the roe –
My heart's in the Highlands wherever I go.
Farewell to the Highlands, farewell to the North!
The birthplace of valour, the country of worth;
Wherever I wander, wherever I rove,
The hills of the Highlands for ever I love.
Farewell to the mountains high covered with snow!
Farewell to the straths and green valleys below!

Farewell to the forests and wild-hanging woods!
Farewell to the torrents and loud-pouring floods!
My heart's in the Highlands, my heart is not here,
My heart's in the Highlands a-chasing the deer;
Chasing the wild deer, and following the roe –
My heart's in the Highlands wherever I go. (14)

The corks were all a-popping and champagne was flowing and being glassed all around the room. As Robbie finished singing and took his glass in hand the countdown began:

"10,9,8,7,6,5,4,3,2,1 – HAPPY NEW YEAR!"

We all stood, shoulder to shoulder with our arms around one another and began to sing:

AULD LANG SYNE

Should auld acquaintance be forgot,
And never brought to mind?
Should auld acquaintance be forgot,
And auld lang syne?
Cho – For auld lang syne, my dear,
For auld lang syne,
We'll tak a cup o' kindness yet
For auld lang syne!
And surely ye'll be your pint-stowp,
And surely I'll be mine,
And we'll tak a cup o'kindness yet
For auld lang syne!
Cho – For auld lang syne, my dear,
For auld lang syne,
We'll tak a cup o' kindness yet
For auld lang syne!
We twa hae run about the braes
And pou'd the gowans fine,
But we've wandered monie a weary fit
Sin' auld lang syne.
Cho – For auld lang syne, my dear,

For auld lang syne,
We'll tak a cup o' kindness yet
For auld lang syne!
We twa hae paidl'd in the burn
Frae morning sun til dine,
But seas between us braid hae roared
Sin' auld lang syne.
Cho – For auld lang syne, my dear,
For auld lang syne,
We'll tak a cup o'kindness yet
For auld lang syne! (15)

Robbie began to fade although he was still watching our serenade. He returned, and then faded a little more.

We continued singing – for it was the greatest compliment we could pay to him. To love his work, to feel and understand the emotions he felt when he wrote "Auld Lang Syne." It was a tradition for us and would always be. Robbie Burns had made a place in all our hearts forever.

I hope you will want to know more about Robbie Burns. I applaud the following:

On The Death of a Favourite Child
The Rights of Woman
Tam o'Shanter
To a Mountain Daisy
The Poet's Welcome to His Love-Begotten Auld Lang Syne
The Young Highland Rover
Lament
A Bard's Epitaph
A Winter Night
Epigram Addressed to an Artist
Her Answer
Winter: A Dirge
I Love My Love in Secret
Line's On the Author's Death
Yon Wild Mossy Mountains

On the Seas and Far Away
A Vision
The Winter of Life
A Fiddler In The North
A Dedication
Anna, Thy Charms
Castle Gordon
Go On, Sweet Bird, And Sooth My Care
How Long and Dreary Is The Night
Lines On The Author's Death
Man Was Made To Mourn: A Dirge
Nature's Law – A Poem.

Beannachd leat!
Cathy McGough
Your Interviewer of Legendary Writers From Beyond

Chapter Seven

TWAIN EXPLAINS WHAT'S IN A NAME

G'day everyone! Before our honoured guest arrives, I just want to take a moment to reveal something to you.

Before I started preparing for this interview, I knew nothing about Mark Twain. I thought I knew about him - having read: "The Prince and the Pauper", "The Adventures of Tom Sawyer", "Huckleberry Finn" and "Pudd'n'head Wilson." I thought I understood the man behind those books, but I was wrong.

I will not go into details regarding Mark Twain's personal life here, but before he arrives, I must tell you that unless you read about the man, you cannot possibly understand his writings. True, you may get a surface kind of understanding, but you will not be able to see that he was more than just America's greatest jester. He was also one of America's most profound philosophers.

Samuel Langhorne Clemens was born on November 30, 1835, in Florida, Missouri. Before he was thirty years old, he saw many grave injustices, which a young boy should never be a witness to. Tragedy surrounded Mr. Twain in his personal life and through the cruelties he saw in the world around him. By then he was so disgusted with life that he put a loaded pistol to his head, but found he lacked the courage to pull the trigger. (1)

As I pondered what the world would have missed if Mr. Twain had taken his life –

I looked up and saw him walking towards me. He wore a white pantsuit, with a white wide-rimmed chapeau and brown shoes. In his right hand he carried an unlit pipe, and his eyes captivated me with their gentleness. I extended my hand, welcoming him for the second time to Sydney, Australia. (His first visit was on September 15, 1885.) (2)

He tipped his hat to me, and then leaned upon the balcony taking in the view. He listened for his old friend the magpie, and then took a seat along side of me. I offered him a large refreshing Mint Julep. He sipped it, clearly savouring the contents.

Q: Is there a place in Australia, which captured your imagination?

A: Without hesitation, The Blue Mountains. Accurately named. "My word!" as the Australians say, but it was a stunning colour that blue. Deep, strong, rich, exquisite; towering and majestic masses of blue - a softly luminous blue, a smouldering blue, as if vaguely lit by fires within. It extinguished the blue of the sky - made it pallid and unwholesome, whitey and washed-out. A wonderful colour - just divine.

A resident told me that those were not mountains; he said they were rabbit-piles. And explained that long exposure and the over-ripe condition of the rabbits was what made them look so blue.

This man may have been right, but much reading of books of travel has made me distrustful of gratis information furnished by unofficial residents of a country. The facts which such people give to travellers are usually erroneous, and often intemperately so. The rabbit-plague has indeed been very bad in Australia, and it could account for one mountain, but not for a mountain range, it seems to me. It is too large an order. (3)

Q: Anything else you'd like to mention?

A: Yes, indeed! The Melbourne Cup - the Australasian National Day. It would be difficult to overstate its importance. It overshadows all other holidays and specialized days of whatever sort in that congeries of colonies. Overshadows them? I might almost say it blots them out.

Each of them gets attention, but not everybody's; each of them evokes interest, but not everybody's; each of them rouses enthusiasm, but not everybody's; in each case a part of the attention, interest, and enthusiasm is a matter of habit and custom, and another part of it is official and perfunctory. Cup Day, and Cup Day only, commands an attention, an interest, and an enthusiasm, which are universal - and spontaneous, not perfunctory.

Cup Day is supreme it has no rival. I can call to mind no specialized annual day, in any country, which can be named by that large name - Supreme. I can call to mind no specialized annual day, in any country, whose approach fires the whole land with a conflagration of conversation and preparation and anticipation and jubilation. No day save this one; but this one does it. (4)

Q: How did you choose your name?

A: I wanted something brief, crisp, definite, unforgettable. I tried over a good many combinations, but none seemed convincing. Then -- in 1863 -- news came to me that an old pilot I once knew, Isaiah Sellers, was dead. At once, the pen name of Captain Sellers occurred to me. That was it; that was the sort of name I wanted. It was not trivial; it had all the right qualities -- Sellers would never need it again. With that line of thinking, the name Mark Twain came to me. It was an old river term, a lead-man's call, signifying two fathoms -- twelve feet. It had richness about it; it was always a pleasant sound for a pilot to hear on a dark night; it meant safe water. (5)

Q: You travelled the world over, what place or thing made the greatest impression upon you?

A: The tomb of Adam! How touching it was, in the land of strangers, far away from home and friends and all who cared for me, thus, to discover the grave of a blood relation. True, a distant one, but still a relation. The unerring instinct of nature thrilled its recognition. The fountain of my filial affection was stirred to its profoundest depths, and I gave way to tumultuous emotion. I leaned upon a pillar and burst into tears. I deem it no shame to have wept over the grave of my poor dead relative. Let him who would sneer at my emotion, visit the Holy Land himself and see how his emotions are affected. (6)

Q: Tom learned a valuable lesson on the Saturday his Aunt Polly made him whitewash her fence. Would you mind reading that passage for us?

A: Ah yes, Tom, always an enterprising lad:

THE ADVENTURES OF TOM SAWYER

Tom said to himself that it was not such a hollow world after all. He had discovered a great law of human action, without knowing it, namely, that, in order to make a man or a boy covet a thing, it is only necessary to make the thing difficult to attain. If he had been a great and wise philosopher, like the writer of this book, he would now have comprehended that work consists of whatever a body is obliged to do, and that play consists of whatever a body is not obliged to do. And this would help him to understand why constructing artificial flowers, or performing on a treadmill, is work, whilst rolling ninepins or climbing Mont Blanc is only amusement. There are wealthy gentlemen in England who drive four-horse passenger-coaches twenty or thirty miles on a daily line, in the summer, because the privilege costs them considerable money; but if they were offered wages for the service that would turn into work, then they would resign. (7)

Q: My son is just about to begin his first year of school. Have you any advice for him?

A: Tell him, when a bully wants to fight him, to take off his coat, slowly and deliberately, and look him straight in the eye. Then still slowly, and deliberately, take off his vest. Then roll up his sleeves and keep on looking him straight in the eye. And if by this time his opponent hasn't run away, then he'd better run himself. (8)

Q: What a treasure you created in the character Pudd'n'head Wilson, so full of humour and wisdom. Do you have a favourite quote from that book?

A: There is no character, howsoever good and fine, but it can be destroyed by ridicule, howsoever poor and witless. Observe the ass, for instance: his character is about perfect, he is the choicest spirit among all the humbler animals yet see what ridicule has brought him to. Instead of feeling complimented, when we are called an ass, we are left in doubt. (9)

Q: I discovered a hard-hitting anti-war poem in your collection. Please explain how you came to write it?

A: The story of mankind is little more than a summary of human bloodshed. First came a long series of unknown wars, murders, and massacres... Next came the Assyrian wars... Next, we had Egyptian wars, Greek wars, Roman wars, hideous drenchings of the earth with blood...And always we had wars, more wars – all over Europe, all over the world. Sometimes in the private interest of royal families, sometimes to crush a weak nation; but never a war started by an aggressor for any clean purpose – there is no such war in the history of the race. (10)

Q: Would you mind reading it for us?

A: I know it by heart:

THE WAR PRAYER

O Lord our God, help us to tear their soldiers to bloody shreds with our shells; help us to cover their smiling fields with the pale forms of their patriot dead; help us to drown the thunder of the guns with the cries of their wounded, writhing in pain; help us to lay waste their humble homes with a hurricane of fire; help us to wring the hearts of their unoffending widows with unavailing grief; help us to turn them out roofless with their little children to wander unfriended through wastes of their desolated land in rags and hunger and thirst, sport of the sun-flames of summer and the icy winds of winter, broken in spirit, worn with travail, imploring Thee for the refuge of the grave and denied it – for our sakes who adore Thee, Lord, blast their hopes, blight their lives, protect their bitter pilgrimage, make heavy their steps, water their way with tears, stain the white snow with the blood of their wounded feet! Grant our prayer, O Lord, and Thine shall be the praise and glory now and forever, Amen. (11)

Q: What is the quickest way to capture an author's heart?

A: There are three infallible ways of pleasing an author, the three form a rising scale of compliment: 1. to tell him that you have read one of his books; 2. to tell him you have read all of his books; 3. to ask him to let you read the manuscript of his forthcoming book. No. 1 admits you to his respect; No. 2 admits you to his admiration; No. 3 carries you clear into his heart. (12)

Q: Do you feel that Horace was right in saying "No writer can make others weep who has not wept himself"? (13)

A: Words, realise nothing, vivify nothing to you, unless you have suffered in your own person the thing, which the words try to describe. (14)

Q: Do you have any advice you would like to offer to writers from the year 2003 and beyond?

A: Use plain, simple language, short words and brief sentences. That is the way to write English - it is the modern way and the best way. Stick to it; don't let fluff and flowers and verbosity creep in. When you catch an adjective, kill it. No, I don't mean utterly, but kill most of them - then the rest will be valuable. They weaken when they are close together. They give strength when they are wide apart. An adjective habit, or a wordy, diffuse, flowery habit, once fastened upon a person, is as hard to get rid of as any other vice. (15)

Q: I believe you have a fable to demonstrate your point?

A: Yes, yes indeed I do!

A FABLE

Once upon a time an artist who had painted a small and very beautiful picture placed it so that he could see it in the mirror. He said, "This doubles the distance and softens it, and it is twice as lovely as it was before."

The animals out in the woods heard of this through the housecat, who was greatly admired by them because he was so learned, and so refined and civilised, and so polite and highbred, and could tell them so much which they didn't know before, and were not certain about afterward. They were much excited about this new piece of gossip, and they asked questions, so as to get at a full understanding of it. They asked what a picture was, and the cat explained.

"It is a flat thing," he said; "wonderfully flat, marvellously flat, enchantingly flat and elegant. And oh, so, beautiful!"

That excited them almost to a frenzy and they said they would give the world to see it.

Then the bear asked, "What is it that makes it so beautiful?"

"It is the looks of it," said the cat.

This filled them with admiration and uncertainty, and they were more excited than ever.

Then the cow asked, "What is a mirror?"

"It is a hole in the wall," said the cat. "You look in it, and there you see the picture, and it is so dainty and charming and ethereal and inspiring in its unimaginable beauty that your head turns round and round, and you almost swoon with ecstasy."

The ass had not said anything as yet; he now began to throw doubts. He said there had never been anything so beautiful as this before, and probably wasn't now. He said that when it took a whole basketful of sesquipedalian adjectives to whoop up a thing of beauty, it was time for suspicion.

It was easy to see that these doubts were having an effect upon the animals, so the cat went off offended. The subject was dropped for a couple of days, but in the meantime, curiosity was taking a fresh start, and there was a revival of interest perceptible. Then the animals assailed the ass for spoiling what could possibly have been a pleasure to them, on a mere suspicion that the picture was not beautiful, without any evidence that such was the case. The ass was not troubled; he was calm and said there was one way to find out who was in the right, himself, or the cat: he would go and look in that hole and come back and tell what he found there. The animals felt relieved and grateful, and asked him to go at once – which he did.

But he did not know where he ought to stand; and so, through error, he stood between the picture and the mirror. The result was that the picture had no chance and didn't show up.

He returned home and said, "The cat lied. There was nothing in that hole but an ass. There wasn't a sign of a flat thing visible. It was a handsome ass, and friendly, but just an ass and nothing more."

The elephant asked, "Did you see it good and clear? Were you close to it?"

"I saw it good and clear, O Hathi, King of Beasts. I was so close that I touched noses with it."

"This if very strange," said the elephant; "the cat was always truthful before – as far as we could make out. Let another witness try. Go, Baloo, look in the hole and come and report."

So, the bear went. When he came back, he said, "Both the cat and the ass have lied; there was nothing in the hole but a bear."

Great was the surprise and puzzlement of the animals. Each was now anxious to make the test himself and get at the straight truth. The elephant sent them one at a time.

First the cow. She found nothing in the hole but a cow.

The tiger found nothing in it but a tiger.

The lion found nothing in it but a lion.

The leopard found nothing in it but a leopard.

The camel found a camel, and nothing more.

Then Hathi was wroth, and said he would have the truth, if he had to go and fetch it himself. When he returned, he abused his whole subjectry for liars, and was in an unappeasable fury with the moral and mental blindness of the cat. He said that anybody, but a nearsighted fool could see that there was nothing in the hole but an elephant.

MORAL, BY THE CAT

You can find in a text whatever you bring if you will stand between it and the mirror of your imagination. You may not see your ears, but they will be there. (16)

As he finished, Mr. Twain began to leave me. I wanted to tell him about his star on "Writer's Walk" at Circular Quay. I told him briefly, as he faded in and out. I wanted to say more – unfortunately, he disappeared. *The following works receive my highest praise:*

Following The Equator

The Adventures of Tom Sawyer

Life On The Mississippi

The Innocents Abroad

The Prince and the Pauper

Pudd'n'head Wilson

Adam's Diary
The Mysterious Stranger
A Connecticut Yankee In King Author's Court
Is Shakespeare Dead?
A Monument to Adam
A Humane Word from Satan
How to Tell a Story
My First Lie and How I Got Out of It
The Man That Corrupted Hadleyburg
Was it Heaven? Or Hell?
See ya!
Cathy McGough
Your Interviewer of Legendary Writers From Beyond

Chapter Eight

COLERIDGE AND PASSION FRUIT

HELLO ONE AND ALL! Today, we are going to meet Samuel Taylor Coleridge, who was born on October 21, 1772. Samuel was the youngest son of the Rector of Ottery, St. Mary's in Devonshire, England.

Mr. Coleridge is a rare writer, because he possessed the remarkable combination of the philosopher, the critic, and the poet all rolled into one. As a philosopher and critic, Mr. Coleridge was able to see results from his labour instantaneously. However, as a poet, Mr. Coleridge had to wait for his Muse to offer up inspiration.

As a Poet, Mr. Coleridge has been referred to as "the apostle of beauty" (1), which is a rather daunting title for anyone to live up to.

Mr. Coleridge achieved this status through writing stanzas like those in old popular ballads such as "The Rime of the Ancient Mariner." It was told in seven parts, and many even today view it as his greatest masterpiece.

While we await his arrival, I will read Part III of the poem for you:

THE RIME OF THE ANCIENT MARINER

Are those her ribs through which the Sun
Did peer, as through a grate?
And is that Woman all her crew?
Is that a Death? And are there two?
Is Death that woman's mate?

Her lips were red, her looks were free,
Her locks were yellow as gold:
Her skin as white as leprosy,
The Night-mare Life-in Death was she,
Who thick's man's blood with cold.

The naked hulk alongside came,
And the twain were casting dice;
'The game is done! I've won! I've won!'
Quoth she, and whistles thrice. (2)

I looked up from my blue hardcover book of treasures, to find Samuel Taylor Coleridge walking through my living room where he joined me on our patio.

He was not tall, but stout, and had very dark hair. I recalled reading that Mr. Coleridge had once described himself as a "great sloth." (3)

As he made his way across the room, I felt he had done himself a grave injustice. Mr. Coleridge didn't dress with flair – but he had a lovable gentleness about him – like a teddy bear.

We exchanged hellos and I offered him a seat. He expressed his preference, which was to amble around the garden.

I encouraged him, pointing out ripe passion fruit, which were heavy on their vine.

He seemed fascinated by them and took one into his hands and cupped it like it was precious. He sniffed it and turned it over.

I asked if he would like to taste it and hurried into the kitchen for a knife and cutting board.

He placed the fruit upon the board and seemed quite interested at first, but when I cut it in half – he lost his desire. He looked at the large black seeds amongst the yellowish pulp and turned away in disgust.

That being finished, he moved around the garden with his hands clasped behind his back for a short while, and then turned abruptly in my direction where he awaited my first question.

Q: Mr. Coleridge, what were you like as a child?

A: As a child I always played alone. I acted out books, pretending I was a hero like King Arthur or Hamlet or Robinson Crusoe. (4)

Q: Your life became lonelier and more difficult when your father died, and you were sent to live with your Uncle. Would you like to share any memories from that period?

A: My Uncle sent me to Christ's Hospital, a famous charity school for blue coat scholars. Every morning, a bit of dry bread and some bad smelling beer. Every evening, a large piece of bread and cheese or butter.... Excepting on Wednesdays, I never had a belly full. Our appetites were damped, never satisfied; we had no vegetables.

The days, the most difficult days were vacation days. Family and friends would visit. Those who remained behind, those who were without family or friends endured a day when the gates were closed from morning until night-time. On a rare occasion I would escape into London on my own and hide in the markets waiting for the time to pass. (5)

Q: Who was "Silas Titus Comberbach"?

A: Silas Titus Comberbach was a name that I invented during my second year at Cambridge. I decided to enlist with a regiment of dragoons. It was not for me. I was a most awkward horseman and couldn't keep astride the saddle. I could not even clean my horse properly and lost most of my equipment. Even my carbine grew rusty. But my messmates did not seem to mind because I told them stories and poems. Then one day, I was scrubbing my horse in the stable and found a piece of chalk. I wrote a Latin inscription on the wall. An officer saw what I had written and appointed me as his orderly. My duty then, was to walk behind my officer in the streets. Unfortunately, someone from Cambridge recognised me, and reported me. That was the end of Silas Titus Comberbach. (6)

Q: When "The Rime of the Ancient Mariner" was published, its content and style scared many readers silly. A critic wrote that it came from "no normal mind." Could you explain what was written in "The Morning Post"?

Mr. Coleridge laughed, sat down beside me and put his hand to his chin and then said:

A: One of the critics from "The Morning Post" wrote: "Here is a nightmare known only to a man in a fainting fit when the blood turns cold and the sweat melts silently from his limbs."

It was clear to me that many readers could not comprehend it, and one sent an anonymous stanza to the paper, which read:

"Your poem must eternal be,
Dear Sir! It cannot fail,
For 'tis incomprehensible,
And without head or tail."

A friend of mine brought the newspaper to me, angered asking, "Who the devil could have sent this in?" I looked deep into his eyes and said, "I did." The two of us then fell about the room laughing. And so, the moral is, in order to fool a critic, BE a critic! (7)

Q: Or you could just ignore them and hope they go away! You certainly wouldn't want them to have the power to make you give up writing to try your hand at something else, like maybe preaching, would you? I am hinting at your short-lived vocation as Minister in Bath.

A: There were seventeen people in the chapel, and when I had scarcely begun one of them stole quietly out of the chapel. A few minutes later another, and then another and then another and then another. When the sermon was over there was no one left but one older woman. She was sound asleep. I decided to find another way to earn bread and cheese. (8)

Q: Would you consider reading something for me?

A: Certainly, dear lady:

KUBLA KHAN

In Xanadu did Kubla Khan
A stately pleasure-dome decree;

Where Alph, the sacred river, ran
Through caverns measureless to man
Down to a sunless sea.
So twice five miles of fertile ground
With walls and towers were girdled round
And here were gardens bright with sinuous rills,
Where blossomed many an incense-bearing tree
And here were forests ancient as the hills,
Enfolding sunny spots of greenery

But oh! That deep romantic chasm which slanted
Down the green hill athwart a cedarn cover!
A savage place! As holy and enchanted
As e'er beneath a waning moon was haunted
By woman wailing for her demon-lover!
And from this chasm, with ceaseless turmoil seething,
As if this earth in fast thick pants were breathing,
A mighty fountain momently was forced;
Amid whose swift half-intermitted burst
Huge fragments vaulted like rebounding hail,
Or chaffy grain beneath the thresher's flail;
And 'mid these dancing rocks at once and ever
It flung up momently the sacred river;
Five miles meandering with a mazy motion
Through wood and dale the sacred river ran,
Then reached the caverns measureless to man,

And sank in tumult to a lifeless ocean;
And 'mid this tumult Kubla heard from far
Ancestral voices prophesying war!

The shadow of the dome of pleasure
Floated midway on the waves;
Where was heard the mingled measure
From the fountain and the caves.
It was a miracle of rare device,
A sunny pleasure-dome with caves of ice!
A damsel with a dulcimer
In a vision once I saw;
It was an Abyssinian maid,
And on the dulcimer she played,
Singing of Mount Abora
Could I revive within me,
Her symphony and song,
To such a deep delight t'would win me,
That with music loud and long,
I would build that dome in air,
That sunny dome! Those caves of ice!
And all who heard should see them there,
And all should cry Beware! Beware!
His flashing eyes, his floating hair!
And close your eyes with holy dread,
For he on honey-dew hath fed,
And drunk the milk of Paradise. (9)

Q: Do you have any advice for poets in the year 2003 and beyond?

A: Poetry must not only be simple, it must also be magical. The poet must delve down into the deep cisterns of his subconscious and send bubbling into the healthy sunshine of the world of normal experience the Crystal Rivers of his fancy reflecting the landscape of a supernatural as well as natural world. A poem is that species of composition, which is opposed to works of science, by proposing for its immediate object pleasure, not truth; and from all other species (having this object in common with it) – it is discriminated by proposing to itself such delight from the whole, as is compatible with a distinct gratification from each component part. Good Sense is the Body of poetic genius, fancy its Drapery, Motion its Life, and Imagination the soul that is everywhere, and in each; and forms all into one graceful intelligent whole. Every man's language varies, according to the extent of his knowledge, the activity of his faculties and the depth or quickness of his feelings. (10)

Q: Would you mind sharing another poem with us before you leave the year 2003? Thank you for meeting with me.

A: I would like to leave you with hope for when I was amongst you, I never found myself alone within the embracement of rocks and hills...but my spirit careered, drove and eddied like a leaf in autumn; a wild activity of thoughts, imaginations, feelings and impulses of motion rose up within me...The further I ascended from animated nature...the greater in me became the intensity of the feeling for life. Life seemed to me then a universal spirit, that neither had nor could have an opposite. God was everywhere and yet there was room for death? (11)

WORK WITHOUT HOPE

All nature seems at work. Slugs leave their
lair –
The bees are stirring – birds are on the
wing –

And Winter slumbering in the open air,
Wears on his smiling face a dream of
Spring!
And I the while, the sole unbusy thing,
Nor honey make, nor pair, nor build, nor
sing

Yet well I ken the banks where amaranths
blow,
Have traced the fount whence streams of
nectar flow,
Bloom, O ye amaranths! Bloom for whom ye
may,
For me ye bloom not! Glide, rich streams,
away!
With lips unbrightened, wreathless brow, I
stroll:
And would you learn the spells that drowse
my soul?
Work without Hope draws nectar in a sieve,
And hope without an object cannot live.
(12)

Samuel Taylor Coleridge picked up a passion fruit in each hand and indicated that he would like to take them with him. I nodded in approval. He carefully placed one in each of his pocket and somehow, I knew that he carried them with him as mementoes of on his journey. In his honour I recited the sweet words of:

ASRA

To be beloved is all I need,
And whom I love I love indeed. (13)

I personally endorse the following works by Samuel Taylor Coleridge:

Christabel
Love
Youth and Age
Dejection: an Ode
The Piccolomini
Ode to Tranquillity
Ode to the Departing Year
Frost at Midnight
Biographia Literaria: 1817
Reflections on Having Left a Place of Retirement
The Lime-Tree Bower, My Prison
The Dungeon
Fears in Solitude
The Pains of Sleep
Phantom
What is Life?
Inscription for a Fountain on a Heath
Human Life
Time, Real and Imaginary
Reason
Desire

Beod ge gesunde

Cathy McGough
Your Interviewer of Legendary Writers From Beyond

Chapter Nine

NATHANIEL HAWTHORNE TURNS THE TABLES

Madame Delatour was very ill. Her personal physician – Dr. Weinstein made a house call in which he ordered her to take some serious R&R.

Having a reluctant patient on my hands, I informed Blanchetta that Dr. Weinstein had left me in charge of her. (Note: if you have to tell your patient that you are in charge then you can always expect trouble!) Therefore, we would not be doing any of our scheduled interviews including the one with Mr. Nathaniel Hawthorne until she was fully recovered.

"Ha!" she exclaimed and then added, "the Show must go on!" and then she went off into a rousing chorus of Freddie Mercury's song of the same name. It wasn't long before she started coughing and sputtering and eventually hacked her way over to the sofa where she reclined with her head in her hands.

There she was, adorned in her furry pink Ugg boots, with a to-the-floor burgundy dressing gown fastened at the top of her neck, her hair under a psychedelic bathing cap, sans makeup apart from a thick slathering of bright red lipstick.

If you came upon her unexpectedly in that state, you might have thought that you had entered into Mr. Serlings' "Twilight Zone." If you listened carefully you probably would have heard, "Do, do do do, Do, do, do, do." In fact, I bet you are hearing the theme from the show right now.

Back to our patient…it was at that time when I offered Madame a nice cool glass of water to ease her fever. She shooed me away and demanded instead a large shot of Chivas Regal on ice. I expressed my concern for her unhealthy choice of beverages since Dr. Weinstein had all but forbidden alcohol.

At last, we reached a compromise: a single watered-down shot with plenty of ice.

After that she reclined on the chaise lounge, sipping with her baby finger in the air attempting to gather up enough strength to enter the world beyond.

Alas, she soon realized that she was still far too weak and begged for another shot. I agreed with extreme reluctance.

After knocking it back, she somewhat unsteadily climbed the stairs where she said she'd rest quietly and gather her strength.

I spied a full bottle of booze under her arm and confiscated it before sending her on her way upstairs for a lie in. Meanwhile, I took advantage of the peace and quiet by perusing the information I had accumulated over time on our interviewer to be Mr. Nathaniel Hawthorne.

Mr. Hawthorne was born in Salem, Massachusetts on July 4th, 1804. His father died when he was four years old, leaving his mother to raise him and his two sisters Elizabeth and Maria. Mrs. Hawthorne being distraught after her husband's death whisked her three children away to her father's home.

Her brother Robert took an interest in Nathaniel and took it upon himself to educate his nephew.

I looked out at the night sky, and one of Mr. Hawthorne's poems came to mind:

ADDRESS TO THE MOON

How sweet the silver Moon's pale ray,
Falls trembling on the distant bay,
O'er which the breezes sigh no more,
Nor billows lash the sounding shore.
Say, do the eyes of those I love,
Behold thee as thou soar'st above,
Lonely, majestic and serene,
The calm and placid evening's Queen?
Say, if upon thy peaceful breast,
Departed spirits find their rest,
For who would wish a fairer home,
Than in that bright, refulgent dome? (1)

I shivered and turned just in time to hear Blanchetta's voice calling me from upstairs: "Yoo-hoo, Cathy, Mr. Hawthorne is on his way."

He had a deep chocolate moustache with flecks of grey in it and long undulating hair. His forehead was masked by a little curl and his dark heavy eyebrows seemed to bring out the dark blue colour of his eyes.

He extended his hand to me, then took my other hand into his and held fast as he looked into my eyes. It felt as if he was trying to read me.

After a few seconds, he took in a deep breath, bowed and then expressed concern for Madame Delatour. I assured him that she had been seen to by a doctor and would be fine if she followed his orders.

Then quite unexpectedly Mr. Hawthorne asked:

Q: You are a budding writer I understand?

A: Yes, Mr. Hawthorne.

Q: Then here is my advice for you, and this is the most important advice that I can give you. Listen carefully - this may be all I have to offer you.

When he casts his leaves forth upon the wind, the author addresses, not the many who will fling aside his volume, or never take it up, but the few who will understand him, better than most of his schoolmates or life mates.

Some authors, indeed, do far more than this, and indulge themselves in such confidential depths of revelation as could fittingly be addressed only and exclusively, to the one heart and mind of perfect sympathy; as if the printed book, thrown at large on the wide world, were certain to find out the divided segment of the writer's own nature, and complete his circle of existence by bringing him into communion with it.

But as thoughts are frozen and utterance benumbed unless the speaker stand in some true relation with his audience, it may be pardonable to imagine that a friend, a kind and apprehensive, though not the closest friend is listening to our talk; and then, a native reserve being thawed by this genial consciousness, we may prate of the circumstances that lie around us, and even of yourself, but still keep the inmost Me behind its veil. To this extent, and within these limits, an author, methinks, may be autobiographical, without violating either the reader's rights or his own. (2)

Q: Thank you Mr. Hawthorne, you have given me much to ponder. Now, if you'd like to have a glass of lemonade and sit down, could we please begin the interview?

A: I am satisfied Cathy. The floor is yours therefore you may proceed.

Q: Is it true that you read "The Pilgrim's Progress" at a very young age?

A: It was a joy to read that book and others when I was six years old. My father died when I was four and learning to read opened a whole new world for me. I loved "The Pilgrim's Progress" and "Castle of Indolence" by James Thomson brought me special delight. I read Spenser's "Faerie Queene" which I purchased with the first money I had ever earned. (3)

Q: What time in your life do you remember with the utmost fondness?

A: When I was fourteen, we moved to Sebago Lake in Maine. I lived like a bird of the air, so perfect was the freedom I enjoyed...Ah, how well I recall the summer days; also, when, with my gun, I roamed at will through the woods of Maine! Everything is beautiful in youth - for all things are allowed to it then...Though it was there I first got my cursed habits of solitude. (4)

Q: Every writer needs solitude, but as a child you do not recommend it?

A: Recommend? No. However, this loneliness I felt as a child forced me to read everything I could find. I read "The Waverley Novels," Rousseau, and "The Newgate Calendar," and I used to invent long stories, about what I wanted to do and where I wanted to go when I grew up. I always concluded my stories with and I'm never coming back again! (5)

Q: Is it true that you started your own newspaper when you were a boy?

A: I did, indeed I did. I called it "The Spectator" - not too original is it? It lasted for a mere six issues and then I informed my subscribers - of which there was one – myself - that no deaths of any importance had taken place, except that of the publisher of said paper who died of starvation, owing to the slenderness of his patronage. (6)

Q: How and when did you decide to become a writer?

A: At seventeen I entered Bowdoin College. I wrote to my mother:

I do not want to be a doctor and live by men's diseases; nor a minister, to live by their sins; nor a lawyer, and live by their quarrels. So, I don't see that there is anything left for me but to be an author. How would you like some day to see a whole shelf full of books written by your son, with "Hawthorne's Works" printed on their backs?

I did not see her response, when she received my letter but later, I knew for certain she was not impressed with my career choice. (7)

Q: Did you feel you could prove your family wrong, or was there any hope for changing their preconceived ideas about you?

A: No aim that I have ever cherished would they recognize as laudable; no success of mine – if my life, beyond its domestic scope, had ever been brightened by success – would they deem otherwise than worthless, if not positively disgraceful. "What is he?" murmurs one grey shadow of my forefathers to the other. "A writer of storybooks! What kind of a business in life – what mode of glorifying God, or being serviceable to mankind in his day and generation – may that be? Why, the degenerate fellow might as well have been a fiddler!" Such are the compliments bandied between my great-grandsires and myself, across the gulf of time! And yet, let them scorn me as they will, strong traits of their nature have intertwined themselves with mine. (8)

Q: All writers receive rejections. How did you handle said rejections, if there were any?

A: If there were any? You jest? In my college days, I wrote poems and sketches. I put them together and called them "Seven Tales of My Native Land." I offered them to publisher #1. They politely turned it down. I offered them to publisher #2. who impolitely turned it down. Publisher #3 who accepted it and kept it for so long without publishing that I demanded they return it to me. How did I handle rejection indeed? I burned the thing! (9)

Q: Oh my, that must've hurt. Did you consider throwing in the towel?

A: I'm not familiar with that phrase but get the gist of what you mean. Therefore, my answer is no. I wrote still and published anonymously at my own expense a novel called "Fanshawe." It cost me $100.00 and sales were few and far between. That being the case, I never publicly admitted I was its author. (10)

Q: Later on, in your life, did you find solace in solitude?

A: I was like a frightened child, even at 38 years of age. I wanted nothing more, than to escape from society. If I saw a man, ambling along, I would scramble hastily over the rocks and take refuge in a nook which many a secret hour has given me a right to call my own. I was like this, until I met my wife Sophia. (11)

Q: You married Sophia on July 9, 1842 and moved to the Old Manse in Concord.

A: It was there I wrote "Mosses." My wife was my sole companion and I needed no other; there was no vacancy in my mind any more than in my heart. In truth, I spent so many years in total seclusion from all human society that it was no wonder that I felt all my desires satisfied by this sole intercourse. But she had come to me from the midst of many friends and a large circle of acquaintance; yet she lived from day to day in the solitude, seeing no one except for myself and later our children, while the snow of our avenue was untrodden for weeks by any footstep save mine; yet she was always so cheerful. Thank God I was able to suffice for her boundless heart! (12)

Q: Concord had quite a reputation in the writing community.

A: We lived on the outskirts where I created stories and lived off the proceeds from them or got by until I was appointed as Surveyor of Customs at Salem in 1846 with a salary of twelve hundred dollars a year. This luck did not last for very long though and in 1849 with a political change I was ousted from my position. I was forty-five years old, with a wife and two children to support. We had very little savings and few prospects for a new position. (13)

Q: You felt the world was against you and then wrote your most famous novel of all "The Scarlet Letter?"

A: Many had faith in me, although I had very little in myself. My wife. My friends from school. My publisher. They all felt I had something in me, to create a great novel. My Publisher James T. Fields came to visit me in Salem. He kindly asked, as he had done many times before, if I had written anything of late. My response was: what publisher would ever risk a book from me, the most unpopular writer in America? He told me that he would with utmost conviction. I answered, that I had nothing worthwhile in my repertoire. Just as he was about to leave, I reached into my desk and pulled out a manuscript, asking if he would like to look over this pile of rubbish. That manuscript was the rough outline of "The Scarlet Letter." (14)

Q: "The Scarlet Letter" was published in 1850 and sold over 5,000 copies in ten days. What did Sophia think of it? Did she like it?

A: I tried to read the conclusion to my wife, for my voice swelled and heaved as if I were tossed up and down on an ocean as it subsides after a storm. It broke her heart – and sent her to bed with a grievous headache - which I looked upon as a triumphant success. (15)

Q: Where did the idea come from?

A: A mysterious package arrived at Custom House and the object, which most drew my attention, was a certain affair of fine red cloth, much worn and faded. There were traces about it of gold embroidery, which, however, was greatly frayed and defaced; so that none, or very little, of the glitter was left. It had been wrought, as was easy to perceive, with wonderful skill of needlework; and the stitch - as I was assured by ladies conversant with such mysteries - gave evidence of a now forgotten art, not to be recovered even by the process of picking out the threads. This rag of scarlet cloth – for time, and wear, and a sacrilegious moth, had reduced it to little other than a rag – on careful examination, assumed the shape of a letter. It was the capital letter "A." (16)

Q: And this "A" what did it look like?

A: By an accurate measurement, each limb proved to be precisely three inches and a quarter in length. It had been intended, there could be no doubt, as an ornamental article of dress; but how it was to be worn, or what rank, honour, and dignity, in by-past times, were signified by it, was a riddle which — so evanescent are the fashions of the world in these particulars — I saw little hope of solving. And yet it strangely interested me. My eyes fastened themselves upon the old scarlet letter and would not be turned aside. Certainly, there was some deep meaning in it, most worthy of interpretation, and which, as it were, streamed forth from the mystic symbol, subtly communicating itself to my sensibilities, but evading the analysis of my mind. (17)

Q: Did the mystery of it all consume you?

A: Yes, while thus perplexed – and cogitating, among other hypotheses, whether the letter might not have been one of those decorations, which the white men used to contrive, in order to take the eyes of Indians – I happened to place it on my breast. It seemed to me – you may smile, but must not doubt my word – it seemed to me then that I experienced a sensation not altogether physical, yet almost so, as of burning heat; and as if the letter were not of red cloth, but red-hot iron. I shuddered and involuntarily let it fall upon the floor.

In the absorbing contemplation of the scarlet letter, I had hitherto neglected to examine a small roll of dingy paper, around which it had been twisted. This I now opened and had the satisfaction to find recorded by the old Surveyor's pen, a reasonably complete explanation of the whole affair. (18)

Q: Was there any specific information, regarding the life of an actual Hester Prynne?

A: Yes, there were several foolscap sheets, containing many particulars respecting the life and conversation of one Hester Prynne, who appeared to have been rather a noteworthy personage in the view of our ancestors. She had flourished during the period between the early days of Massachusetts and the close of the seventeenth century. Aged persons, alive in the time of Mr. Surveyor Pue, and from whose oral testimony he had made up his narrative, remembered her in their youth as a very old, but not decrepit woman, of a stately and solemn aspect. It had been her habit from an almost immemorial date to go about the country as a kind of voluntary nurse, and doing whatever miscellaneous good she might; taking upon herself, like-wise, to give advice in all matters, especially those of the heart; by which means, as a person of such propensities inevitably must, she gained from many people the reverence due to an angel, but I should imagine was looked upon by others as an intruder and a nuisance. (19)

Q: Were there any further discoveries?

A: Prying further into the manuscript I found the record of other doings and sufferings of this singular woman, entitled "The Scarlet Letter" — and it should be borne carefully in mind, that the main facts of that story are authorized and authenticated by the document of Mr. Surveyor Pue. The original papers, together with the scarlet letter itself – a most curious relic – are still in my possession, and shall be freely exhibited to whomsoever, induced by my great interest of the narrative, may desire a sight of them. (20)

Q: So, you knew straightaway this "A" — this information you found was something you wanted to write about?

A: I knew Hester Prynne's story required much thought. So little adapted is the atmosphere of a Custom House to the delicate harvest of fancy and sensibility, that, had I remained there through ten Presidencies yet to come, I doubt whether the tale of "The Scarlet Letter" would ever have been brought before the public eye. My imagination was a tarnished mirror. It would not reflect, or only with miserable dimness, the figures with which I did my best to people it. The characters of the narrative would not be warmed and rendered malleable by any heat that I could kindle at my intellectual forget. They would take neither the glow of passion nor the tenderness of sentiment but retained all the rigidity of dead corpses and started me in the face with a fixed and ghastly grin of contemptuous defiance. (21)

Q: Is it true "The Scarlet Letter" was once made into an opera?

A: Yes, while abroad I picked up an American newspaper. It said that an opera, still unfinished had been written on my book and that several scenes of it had been performed successfully in New York. I should think it might possibly succeed as an opera, though it would certainly fail as a play. (22)

Q: My first book was a Romance. What advice would you give to writers in that specific genre?

A: When a writer calls his work a Romance, it need hardly be observed that he wishes to claim a certain latitude, both as to its fashion and material, which he would not have felt himself entitled to assume had he professed to be writing a Novel. The latter form of composition is presumed to aim at a very minute fidelity, not merely to the possible, but to the probably and ordinary course of man's experience. The former – while, as a work of art, it must rigidly subject itself to laws, and while it sins unpardonably so far as it may swerve aside from the truth of the human heart – has fairly a right to present that truth under circumstances, to a great extent, of the writer's own choosing or creation.

If he thinks fit, also, he may so manage his atmospherical medium as to bring out or mellow the lights and deepen and enrich the shadows of the picture. He will be wise, no doubt, to make a very moderate use of the privileges here stated, and especially, to mingle the Marvellous rather as a slight, delicate, and evanescent flavour, than as any portion of the actual substance of the dish offered to the public. He can hardly be said, however, to commit a literary crime, even if he disregards this caution. (23)

Q: How important do you think a moral purpose is in writing a novel?

A: Many writers lay a very great stress upon some definite Moral purpose, at which they profess to aim their works. Not to be deficient in this particular, the author has provided himself with a moral; - the truth, namely, that the wrong-doing of one generation lives into the successive ones, and divesting itself of every temporary advantage, becomes pure and uncontrollable mischief; and he would feel it singular gratification, if this romance might effectually convince mankind – or indeed, any one man – of the folly of tumbling down an avalanche of ill-gotten gold, or real estate, on the heads of an unfortunate posterity thereby to maim and crush them, until the accumulated mass shall be scattered abroad in its original atoms. (24)

Q: So, you don't think the Romance genre should attempt to educate?

A: When romances do really teach anything, or produce any effective operation, it is usually through a far more subtle process than the ostensible one the author has considered it hardly worth his while, therefore, relentlessly to impale the story with its moral, as with an iron rod – or rather as by sticking a pin through a butterfly – thus at once depriving it of life, and causing it to stiffen in an ungainly and unnatural attitude. A high truth, indeed, fairly, finely, and skilfully wrought out, brightening at every step and crowning the final development of a work of fiction, may add an artistic glory, but is never any truer, and seldom any more evident, at the last page than at the first. (25)

Q: How then should a writer strive to connect with readers?

A: A reader may perhaps choose to assign an actual locality to the imaginary event of the narrative. If permitted by the historical connection – which, though slight, was essential to the writer's plan – the author would very willingly have avoided anything of this nature. Not to speak of other objections, it exposes the romance to an inflexible and exceedingly dangerous species of criticism, by bringing his fancy pictures almost into positive contact with the realities of the moment.

It has been no part of his object, to describe local manners, nor in any way to meddle with the characteristics of a community for whom he cherishes a proper respect and a natural regard. He trusts not to be considered unpardonably offending, by laying out a street that infringes upon nobody's private rights and appropriating a lot of land which had no visible owner and building a house of materials long in use for constructing castles in the air. The personages of the tale – though they give themselves out to be of ancient stability and considerable prominence – are really of the author's own making, or, at all events, of his own mixing; their virtues can shed no lustre, nor their defects redound, in the remotest degree, to the discredit of the venerable town of which they profess to be inhabitants. He would be glad, therefore, if – especially in the quarter to which he alludes – the book may be read strictly as a Romance, having a great deal more to do with the clouds overhead than with any portion of the actual soil of the place which he writes about. (26)

Q: During your travels to Britain what if anything stands out in your mind?

A: I visited the British Museum; an exceedingly tiresome affair. It quite crushes a person to see so much at once; and I wandered from hall to hall with a weary and heavy heart. The present is burdened too much with the past. (27)

Q: Have you any further advice for writers in the future?

A: The only sensible ends of literature are, first, the pleasurable toil of writing; second, the gratification of one's family and friends; and, lastly, the solid cash. (28)

Q: I regret to say that our time is now ending. Thank you so much for agreeing to be interviewed. This book would not be complete without a chapter about you.

A: I humbly thank you and will leave you with a reading from:

THE SCARLET LETTER

When the young woman—the mother of this child—stood fully revealed before the crowd, it seemed to be her first impulse to clasp the infant closely to her bosom; not so much by an impulse of motherly affection, as that she might thereby conceal a certain token, which was wrought or fastened into her dress. In a moment, however, wisely judging that one token of her shame would but poorly serve to hide another, she took the baby on her arm, and with a burning blush, and yet a haughty smile, and a glance that would not be abashed, looked around at her townspeople and neighbours. On the breast of her gown, in fine red cloth, surrounded with elaborate embroidery and fantastic flourishes of gold thread, appeared the letter A. It was so artistically done, and with so much fertility and gorgeous luxuriance of fancy, that it had all the effect of a last and fitting decoration to the apparel which she wore, and which was of a splendour in accordance with the taste of the age, but greatly beyond what was allowed by the sumptuary regulations of the colony. (29)

After he finished reciting, he disappeared, and I continued reading where he had left off for quite some time.

Nathaniel Hawthorne was well respected by his fellow writers who paid tribute to him at his burial including Longfellow, Holmes, Whittier, Lowell, Emerson, Agassiz, and Pierce.

I leave you with these words, written by Henry Wadsworth Longfellow at the time of Mr. Hawthorne's death:

HAWTHORNE [1804-1864]

How beautiful it was, that one bright day
In the long week of rain!
Though all its splendour could not chase away
The omnipresent pain.
The lovely town was white with apple-blooms,
And the great elms o'erhead
Dark shadows wove on their aerial looms
Shot through with golden thread.
Across the meadows, by the grey old manse,
The historic river flowed;
I was as one who wanders in a trance,
Unconscious of his road.
The faces of familiar faces seemed strange;
Their voices I could hear,
And yet the words they uttered seemed to change
Their meaning to my ear.
For the one face I looked for was not there,
The one low voice was mute;
Only an unseen presence filled the air
And baffled my pursuit.
Now I look back, and meadow, manse, and stream
Dimly my thought defines;
I only see—a dream within a dream—
The hill-top hearsed with pines.
I only hear above his place of rest
Their tender undertone,
The infinite longings of a troubled breast,
The voice so like his own.
There in seclusion and remote from men
The wizard hand lies cold,
Which at its topmost speed let fall the pen,
And left the tale half told.
Ah! Who shall lift that wand of magic power,

And the lost clew regain?
The unfinished windows in Aladdin's tower
Unfinished must remain! (30)

My advice is to seek out Mr. Hawthorne's works! You will not be disappointed:

The Scarlet Letter
Twice Told Tales
The Blithedale Romance
The House of the Seven Gables
Rappaccini's Daughter
The Marble Faun
Tanglewood Tales
The Dolliver Romance
Note-books
English Note-books
Our Old Home – A Series of English Sketches
A Whole History of Grandfather's Chair
The Minister's Black Veil
The Artist of the Beautiful
Forms of Heroes
The Prophetic Pictures
The Gentle Boy
Drowne's Wooden Image
Earth's Holocaust
The Devil in Manuscript
The Great Stone Fact
Mr. Higginbotham's Catastrophe
The Procession of Life
The Canterbury Pilgrims.

TTFN!
Cathy McGough
Your Interviewer of Legendary Writers From Beyond

Chapter Ten

LEACOCK CAUSES A STIR

In the autumn of 2000, Madame Delatour and I were touring the Gatineau Hills in Quebec. Leaves were fluttering down and around our car, as we made our way up the hills. The magnificent colours made us long for a place to stop where we could go on walkabout and experience the sights and smells of a Canadian fall season.

At last, we came upon the parking lot, which would lead us to the Continental Shelf. The sounds of leaves crunching and chattering as we made our way towards the look-out point made it necessary for us to shout to communicate. It was a rather cool midday, and there weren't many others who were brave enough to retire from the warmth of their automobiles to go on a sightseeing tour.

We sauntered along a walking trail, while the aromatic mossy pathways assaulted our senses and insulated us from the wind. We discussed Canadian Literature as we ambled along taking it all in and in my mind a poem began:

The crunching leaves under my feet,
Created a rhythmic pulsing in my mind.

Rising then falling - my soles kissed the ground,
Poem in my head going round and round.

Mr. Leacock's voice brought me back to the present time with a recitation from:

THE SOCIAL PLAN

I know a very tiresome Man
Who keeps on saying, "Social Plan."
At every Dinner, every Talk
Where Men foregather, eat or walk,
No matter where, -- this Awful Man
Brings on his god dam Social Plan.
The Fall in Wheat, the Rise in Bread,
The Social Breakers dead ahead,
The Economic Paradox
That drives the Nation on the rocks,
The Wheels that false Abundance clogs --
And frightens us from raising Hogs, --
This dreary field, the Gloomy Man
Surveys and hiccoughs, Social Plan.
Till simpler Men begin to find
His croaking aggravates their mind,
And makes them anxious to avoid
All mention of the Unemployed,
And leads them even to abhor
The People called Deserving Poor.
For me, my sympathies now pass
To the poor Plutocratic Class.
The Crowd that now appeals to me
Is what he calls the Bourgeoisie
So, I have got a Social Plan
To take him by the Neck,
And lock him in a Luggage van
And tie on it a check,
Marked MOSCOW VIA TURKESTAN,

Now, how's that for a Social Plan? (1)

Madame Delatour had no idea who wrote "The Social Plan" but she was thoroughly entertained by it. I told her it was Canada's own Stephen Leacock's work and mentioned he was our finest humourist. Madame Delatour wanted to know why I hadn't asked her to contact Mr. Leacock for an interview.

To be honest, I wasn't sure why we hadn't attempted to speak with him. I suggested we might discuss it further – after I had the opportunity to do some investigating.

Moments later, I noticed a gentleman walking towards us in the distance along the pathway. Madame Delatour shrugged her shoulders at me – stating that Mr. Leacock was willing and able to be interviewed right here, right now.

I was somewhat annoyed since there was no time to do the required preparation, but when you're working with a psycho – oops I meant psychic – you learn to go with the flow.

The rain began to gently fall with occasional drips getting through the gaps left by the semi-leaf-less trees. We ran and held fast with our backs against a huge Maple tree waiting for Mr. Leacock to join us.

He was dressed in a brown comfy cardigan and looked like he would be right at home in a big crunchy La-Z-Boy chair, positioned in front of a roaring fireplace smoking a pipe. He wore brown trousers, matching shoes (which were covered with damp leaves) - and a brown chequered Scottish-like cap. His shoulders were hunched to keep the wind out and his hands were tucked away in the warmth of his cardigan's pockets.

Stephen Leacock was born on December 30, in 1869 in Hampshire, England. He was the third child in a family of eleven children. His family immigrated to Canada in 1876. They bought a 100-acre farm in the Village of Sutton, Ontario.

Mr. Leacock soon joined us under the Maple tree. We had a brief chat about the weather (as is Canadian custom) before proceeding with the interview.

Q: You must have been excited to see your first Canadian home. What do you remember about it?

A: Our farm with its buildings was, I will say, the damnedest place I ever saw. I can remember it, like it was yesterday.

Stinking bars and stables. One sad little candle to study by at night. Oh, and winter nights, freezing cold nights in the house. (2)

Q: You decided to become a teacher?

A: I had at that time a certain natural gift of mimicry, could easily hit off people's voices and instinctively reproduce their gestures. So, when Jimmy Wetherell [the senior instructor], halfway through a lesson in English, said to me most courteously, "Now will you take the lesson over at that point and continue it?" I did so with a completeness and resemblance to Jimmy's voice and manner, which of course delighted the class. Titters ran through the room.

Encouraged as an artist, I laid it on too thick. The kindly Principal saw it himself and flushed pink. When I finished, he said quietly, "I am afraid I admire your brains more than your manners."

The words cut me to the quick. I felt them to be so true and yet so completely without malice. For I had no real "nerve," no real "gall." It was the art of imitation that appealed to me. I had not realized how it might affect the person concerned. I learned with it my first lesson in the need for human kindliness as an element in humour. (3)

Q: A lesson well learned. Still, you pursued a career teaching.

A: To go into teaching was a matter of sheer necessity. My education fitted me for nothing except to pass it on to the other people. (4)

Q: How were you inspired to write "The Social Plan"?

A: Lecturing before a brilliant galaxy of young men and women, known, in the college where they belong, as Economics Three, there occurred to me, and I used, the metaphor of a social reformer sitting as a raven on the window-sill and croaking "Social Plan. Economics Three" woke up and laughed.

This gave me the idea that it might be of great service if economic problems could be discussed in the form of the literature of the imagination. This would help to remove the argument from the angers and the bitterness that so often surround it. If we cannot discuss it like gentlemen, let us at least discuss it like idiots. Having got the idea, all I had to do was to write the poem.

Forty years of hard work on economics has pretty well removed all the ideas I ever had about it. I think the whole science is a wreck and has got to be built up again. For our social problems there is about as much light to be found in the older economics as from a glow-worm.

Only one or two things seem to me clear. Cast-iron communism is nothing but a penitentiary. Sooner or later either it is doomed, or man is doomed. I believe that the only possible basis for organised society is that of every man for himself, -- for himself and those near and dear to him. But on this basis, there must be put in operation a much more efficient and much more just social mechanism. We need not a new game but a new set of rules. There must be bread and work for all; and that ought to mean mighty little work and lots of bread. (5)

Q: Would you mind reading one of your short stories?

A: I was hoping you were going to get around to asking!

MY FINANCIAL CAREER

When I go into a bank I get rattled. The clerks rattle me; the wickets rattle me; the sight of the money rattles me; everything rattles me.

The moment I cross the threshold of a bank and attempt to transact business there, I become an irresponsible idiot.

I knew this beforehand, but my salary had been raised to fifty dollars a month and I felt that the bank was the only place for it.

So, I shambled in and looked timidly round at the clerks. I had an idea that a person about to open an account must need consult the manager.

I went up to a wicket marked "Accountant." The accountant was a tall, cool devil. The very sight of him rattled me. My voice was sepulchral.

"Can I see the manager?" I said, and added solemnly, "alone." I don't know why I said "alone."

"Certainly," said the accountant, and fetched him.

The manager was a grave, calm man. I held my fifty-six dollars clutched in a crumpled ball in my pocket.

"Are you the manager?" I said. God knows I didn't doubt it.

"Yes," he said.

"Can I see you," I asked, "alone?" I didn't want to say "alone" again, but without it the thing seemed self-evident.

The manager looked at me in some alarm. He felt that I had an awful secret to reveal.

"Come in here," he said, and led the way to a private room. He turned the key in the lock.

"We are safe from interruption here," he said, "Sit down."

We both sat down and looked at each other. I found no voice to speak.

"You are one of Pinkerton's men, I presume," he said.

He had gathered from my mysterious manner that I was a detective. I knew what he was thinking, and it made me worse.

"No, not from Pinkerton's," I said, seeming to imply that I came from a rival agency.

"To tell the truth," I went on, as if I had been prompted to lie about it, "I am not a detective at all. I have come to open an account. I intend to keep all my money in this bank."

The manager looked relieved but still serious; he concluded now that I was a son of Baron Rothschild or a young Gould.

"A large account, I suppose," he said.

"Fairly large," I whispered, "I propose to deposit fifty-six dollars now and fifty dollars a month regularly."

The manager got up and opened the door. He called to the accountant.

“Mr. Montgomery,” he said unkindly loud, "this gentleman is opening an account, he will deposit fifty-six dollars. Good morning."

I rose.

A big iron door stood open at the side of the room. "Good morning," I said, and stepped into the safe.

"Come out," said the manager coldly, and showed me the other way.

I went up to the accountant's wicket and poked the ball of money at him with a quick convulsive movement as if I were doing a conjuring trick.

My face was ghastly pale.

"Here," I said, "Deposit it." The tone of the words seemed to mean, "Let us do this painful thing while the fit is on us."

He took the money and gave it to another clerk.

He made me write the sum on a slip and sign my name in a book. I no longer knew what I was doing. The bank swam before my eyes.

"Is it deposited?" I asked in a hollow, vibrating voice.

"It is," said the accountant.

"Then I want to draw a cheque."

My idea was to draw out six dollars of it for present use. Someone gave me a chequebook through a wicket and someone else began telling me how to write it out. The people in the bank had the impression that I was an invalid millionaire. I wrote something on the check and thrust it in at the clerk. He looked at it.

"What! Are you drawing it all out again?" he asked in surprise.

Then I realised that I had written fifty-six instead of six. I was too far-gone to reason now. I had a feeling that it was impossible to explain the thing.

All the clerks had stopped writing to look at me.

Reckless with misery, I made a plunge.

"Yes, the whole thing."

"You withdraw your money from the bank?"

"Every cent of it."

"Are you not going to deposit anymore?" said the clerk, astonished.

"Never."

An idiot hope struck me that they might think something had insulted me while I was writing the check and that I had changed my mind. I made a wretched attempt to look like a man with a fearfully quick temper.

The clerk prepared to pay the money. "How will you have it?" he said.

"What?"

"How will you have it?"

"Oh" - I caught his meaning and answered without even trying to think - "in fifties."

He gave me a fifty-dollar bill.

"And the six?" he asked dryly.

“In sixes," I said.

He gave it me and I rushed out.

As the big door swung behind me, I caught the echo of a roar of laughter that went up to the ceiling of the bank.

Since then I bank no more. I keep my money in cash in my trousers pocket and my savings in silver dollars in a sock. (6)

Mr. Leacock reached into his trouser pockets, pulling out some Canadian bills and jingling a small amount of change. A chipmunk scattered across the pathway, hoping food was on offer - but not a crust of bread was in sight.

Q: Define humour?

A: Humour in its highest meaning and its furthest reach... does not depend on verbal incongruities, or on tricks of sight and hearing. It finds its basis in the incongruity of life itself, and contrast between the fretting cares and the petty sorrows of the day and the long mystery of the tomorrow. Here laughter and tears become one, and humour becomes the contemplation and interpretation of our life. (7)

Q: Have you any advice for wannabe humourists?

A: Do not ever try to be funny, for it is a terrible curse. Here is a world going to pieces and I am worried. Yet when I stand up before an audience to deliver my serious thoughts, they begin laughing. I have been advertised to them as funny, and they refuse to accept me as anything else. (8)

Q: I am fascinated by your studies in education and for the first years of school because my son is in Kindergarten. Would you mind talking about your findings in that area?

A: For many centuries elementary education was largely based on the idea that sparing the rod spoiled the child and that the quickest way to reach the youthful intellect was from below up. But one recalls on the other hand Rousseau's little "Emile" wandering among the flowers, and the rise of the Kindergarten - the children's garden, which has ascended from infancy up throughout our system of education.

I can recall from my own childhood, in England, a little elementary primer called "Reading without Tears." This was regarded at the time as a pleasing innovation. (9)

Q: Perhaps you could explain a little more?

A: In other words, I am trying to say that in much of our education (in practice at least) it is quicker to go from the unknown to the known. To proceed ad obscurum per obscurius is often as useful as to go through a tunnel to save walking round a mountain. (10)

We cannot in our day leave education to the unaided prompting of the individual's desire to know and the individual's self-interest in knowing. Education cannot be left to itself. To a great extent the creative arts of painting, sculpture and music may be left with no further recognition by the state and the law than a generous pecuniary support. But education by obvious necessity must be under the constant care and the detailed regulation of society at large. Whatever shortcomings are involved need to be admitted and faced or mitigated as best we can. (11)

Q: You did the lecture circuit quite a lot. What is your most memorable moment?

A: To one experience of my tour as a lecturer I shall always be able to look back with satisfaction. I nearly had the pleasure of killing a man with laughing: and this in the most literal sense. American lecturers have often dreamed of doing this. I nearly did it.

The man in question was a comfortable apoplectic-looking man with the kind of merry rubicund face that is seen in countries where they don't have prohibition. He was seated near the back of the hall and was laughing uproariously.

Suddenly, I realised that something was happening. The man had collapsed sideways onto the floor; a little group of men gathered about him; they lifted him up and I could see them carrying him out, a silent and inert mass.

As in duty bound, I went right on with my lecture. But my heart beat high with satisfaction. I was sure that I had killed him.

You may judge how high these hopes rose when a moment or two later a note was handed to the chairman who then asked me to pause for a moment in my lecture and stood up and asked, “Is there a doctor in the audience?”

A doctor rose and silently went out.

The lecture continued; but there was no more laughter; my aim had now become to kill another of them, and they knew it. They were aware that if they started laughing, they might die.

In a few minutes a second note was handed to the chairman. He announced very gravely, "A second doctor is wanted." The lecture went on in deeper silence than ever. All the audience were waiting for a third announcement. It came.

A new message was handed to the chairman. He rose and said, "If Mr. Murchison, the undertaker, is in the audience, will he kindly step outside."

That man, I regret to say, got well. (12)

Q: Is there anything worse than having a heckler in the audience?

A: Yes! I find, for example, that wherever I go there is always seated in the audience, about three seats from the front, a silent man with a big motionless face like a melon. He is always there. I have seen that man in every town or city from Richmond, Indiana, to Bournemouth to Hampshire. He haunts me. I get to expect him. I feel like nodding to him from the platform. And I find that all other lecturers have the same experience. Wherever they go the man with the big face is always there. He never laughs; no matter if the people all round him are convulsed with laughter, he sits there like a rock--or, no, like a toad--immovable.

What he thinks I don't know. Why he comes to lectures I cannot guess. (13)

Q: You lectured all over the world. Any impressions you would like to share?

A: I find that I receive impressions with great difficulty and have nothing of that easy facility in picking them up which is shown by British writers on America. I remember Hugh Walpole telling me that he could hardly walk down Broadway without getting at least three dollars' worth and on Fifth Avenue five dollars' worth; and I recollect that St.

John Ervine came up to my house in Montreal, drank a cup of tea, borrowed some tobacco, and got away with sixty dollars' worth of impressions of Canadian life and character. (14)

Q: Perhaps if I narrowed it down for you then? What was your impression of London, England?

A: A far deeper meaning is found in the examination of the great historic monuments of the city. The principal ones of these are the Tower of London, the British Museum and Westminster Abbey.

No visitor to London should fail to see these. Indeed, he ought to feel that his visit to England is wasted unless he has seen them.

I speak strongly on the point because I feel strongly on it.

To my mind there is something about the grim fascination of the historic Tower, the cloistered quiet of the Museum and the majesty of the ancient Abbey, which will make it the regret of my life that I didn't see any one of the three. I fully meant to: but I failed: and I can only hope that the circumstances of my failure may be helpful to other visitors. (15)

Q: You didn't see any of those must-see places? Mr. Leacock, why not?

A: The Tower of London I most certainly intended to inspect. Each day, after the fashion of every tourist, I wrote for myself a little list of things to do and I always put the Tower of London on it. No doubt the reader knows the kind of little list that I mean. It runs:

1. Go to bank.
2. Buy a shirt.
3. National Picture Gallery.
4. Razor blades.
5. Tower of London.
6. Soap.

This itinerary, I regret to say, was never carried out in full. (16)

Q: Perhaps you preferred to blend in – so people couldn't play spot the tourist?

A: Londoners, after all, in not seeing their own wonders, are only like the rest of the world. The people who live in Buffalo never go to see Niagara Falls; people in Cleveland don't know which is Mr. Rockefeller's house, and people live and even die in New York without going up to the top of the Woolworth Building.

And anyway, the past is remote, and the present is near.

I know a cab driver in the city of Quebec whose business in life it is to drive people up to see the Plains of Abraham, but unless they bother him to do it, he doesn't show them the spot where Wolfe fell: what he does point out with real zest is the place where the Mayor and the City Council sat on the wooden platform that they put up for the municipal celebration one summer. (17)

Mr. Leacock started to fade in and out, as the rain began to pelt down upon us like we were in the heart of a storm. He smiled, as he bent down and picked up some crispy maple leaves. He looked at their fiery colours and was clearly amazed how alive they appeared to be even though they were no longer part of the tree. He put them to his nose, and breathed in deeply, taking in the fragrance. A squirrel chitter-chattered above us, trying to capture our attention as Mr. Leacock put the leaves into his pocket and disappeared from my sight.

I ran back to the car, where Madame Delatour had already taken shelter. She was sitting inside with the windows all fogged up listening to "Barry Manilow's Greatest Hits."

Soon we were on our way out of the Gatineau Hills, having been privileged enough to meet Mr. Stephen Leacock at a very unexpected time and place.

Mr. Leacock offers a very extensive list of work including essays on Economics and many other subjects. I hope this interview only whetted your appetite and can personally vouch for the following:

Literary Lapses
Sunshine Sketches of a Little Town
Arcadian Adventures with the Idle Rich
Further Foolishness
Frenzied Fiction
How to Introduce Two People to One Another
Short Circuits
The Dry Pickwick
Last Leaves
My Discovery of England
Humour: Its Theory and Technique,
With Examples and Samples; A Book of Discovery
The Boy I Left Behind Me
The Hallucination of Mr. Butt
My Remarkable Uncle
The Retroactive Existence of Mr. Juggins
The Dawn of Canadian History: A Chronicle of Aboriginal Canada
Moonbeams from the Larger Lunacy
Nonsense Novels
A Discussion of Freedom and Compulsion in Education
Behind The Beyond
Fiction and Reality.

So long until next time!
Cathy McGough
Your Interviewer of Legendary Writers From Beyond

Chapter Eleven

KIPLING DOWN UNDER AGAIN

Another week has passed. My, oh my where has the time gone?

For this week's interview, we are going back in time. Back, back, to the moment when Madame Delatour brought Rudyard Kipling into my home.

Mr. Kipling wrote a poem, which became my anthem during the awkward teenage years. I had it upon the wall of my bedroom on a giant poster and am still able to recite it by heart:

IT CAN BE DONE
IF you can keep your head when all about you
Are losing theirs and blaming it on you,
IF you can trust yourself when all men doubt you,
But make allowance for their doubting too;
IF you can wait and not be tired by waiting,
Or being lied about, don't deal in lies,
Or being hated don't give way to hating,
And yet don't look too good, nor talk too wise:

IF you can dream – and not make dreams your master;
IF you can think – and not make thoughts your aim,
IF you can meet with Triumph and Disaster
And treat those two impostors just the same
IF you can bear to hear the truth you've spoken
Twisted by knaves to make a trap for fools,
Or watch the things you gave your life to, broken,
And stoop and build'em up with worn-out tools;
IF you can make one heap of all your winnings
And risk it on one turn of pitch-and-toss,
And lose, and start again at your beginnings
And never breathe a word about your loss;
IF you can force your heart and nerve and sinew
To serve your turn long after they are gone,
And so hold on when there is nothing in you
Except the Will, which says to them: "Hold on!"
IF you can talk with crowds and keep your virtue,
Or walk with Kings – nor lose the common touch,
IF neither foes nor loving friends can hurt you,
IF all men count with you, but none too much;
IF you can fill the unforgiving minute
With sixty seconds' worth of distance run,
Yours is the Earth and everything that's in it,
And – which is more – you'll be a man my son! (1)

Who cannot - WILL NOT- be inspired by those words?

Rudyard Kipling was born on December 30, 1865, and he spent his childhood in Bombay, India.

Just then, Mr. Kipling came walking onto the balcony and I welcomed him to my home in Sydney, Australia.

I implored him to take a seat and offered him a glass of Australia's finest Port. He accepted a jigger and I poured one for myself and then we toasted to the magpies - our only audience.

Q: How did you come to name your house "Naulahka?"

A: "Naulahka" was taken from a novel I wrote in collaboration with my brother-in-law Wolcott-Balestier. It means "The Jewel." My wife Caroline and I thought the name perfect for the bungalow we had built in Brattleboro, Vermont, in 1892. We lived there very happily for nearly five years. (2)

Q: Have you always enjoyed reading?

A: I was near-sighted from birth yet as a boy I read continuously and omnivorously scores and scores of ancient dramatists...Hakluyt's voyages, French translations of Muscovite authors Pushkin and Lermontov.

When Father and Mother heard I could read they sent me priceless volumes. One I retained all of my life, a bound copy of "Aunt Judy's Magazine" of the early seventies, in which appeared "Mrs. Ewing's Six to Sixteen."

I owe more in circuitous ways to that tale than I can tell. I knew it, as I know it still, almost by heart. Here was a history of real people and real things. It was better than Knatchbull-Hugessen's "Tales at Tea-time." Better even than "The Old Shikari" with its steel engravings of charging pigs and angry tigers.

On another plane was an old magazine with Scott's "I climbed the dark brow of the mighty Helvellyn." I knew nothing of its meaning, but the words moved and pleased. So did other extracts from the poems of A. Tennyson.

When my Father sent me "Robinson Crusoe" with steel engravings I set up in business alone as a trader with savages (the wreck parts of the tale never much interested me), in a mildewy basement room where I stood my solitary confinements. My apparatus was a coconut shell strung on a red cord, a tin trunk, and a piece of packing case -which kept off any other world. Thus, fenced about, everything inside the fence was quite real, but mixed with the smell of damp cupboards. If the bit of board fell, I had to begin the magic all over again. I have learned since from children who play much alone that this rule of beginning again in a pretend game is not uncommon. The magic, you see, lies in the ring or fence that you take refuge in. (3)

Q: I understand you purchased some Canadian land on your honeymoon?

A: Caroline and I were married in the church at Langham Place - Gosse - and a few days afterwards we were on our magic carpet, which was to take us, round the earth, beginning with Canada deep in snow.

Among our wedding gifts was a generous silver flask filled with whiskey, but of incontinent habit. It leaked in the valise where it lay with flannel shirts. And it scented the entire Pullman from end to end ere we arrived at the cause. By that time, all our fellow passengers pitied that poor girl who had linked her life to this shameless inebriate.

Thus, in a false atmosphere all of our innocent own, we came to Vancouver, where with an eye to the future and for proof of wealth we bought, or thought we had, twenty acres of a wilderness called North Vancouver, now part of the city.

But there was a catch in the thing, as we found many years later when, after paying taxes on it forever so long, we discovered it belonged to someone else. All the consolation we got then from the smiling people of Vancouver was:

"You bought that from Steve, did you? Ah-ah, Steve! You hadn't ought to ha' bought from Steve. No! Not from Steve."

And thus did, the good Steve cure us of speculating in real estate. (4)

Q: Please accept my apologies (as a Canadian by birth) for Steve's misappropriation of your funds. Perhaps Steve was an Animal Rights Activist and heard you had a passion for hunting?

A: I went hunting in the woods, not gun hunting but "eye hunting". I loved the woods for their own sake and not for the sake of slaughter. There was nothing quite so glorious as the sun-and-pine-drenched perfume of the New England countryside. Especially in the summer. The New England summer has Creole blood in her veins. (5)

Q: You were a successful Journalist in India, and hoped to continue your career when you relocated to the U.S. However, the Editor of "The Examiner" was not exactly co-operative.

A: I was twenty-four years old and I had been writing for some years. I had already penned "The Man Who Would Be King."

In any case, the Editor told me, "I'm sorry Mr. Kipling, but you just don't know how to use the English language. You'll excuse my bluntness, but "The Examiner" is not a kindergarten for amateur writers. (6)

Q: Ouch, that must've hurt! You were always welcomed and adored in Australia though. In fact, Australia still honours your visit here in 1821, by a plaque on Circular Quay. How do you remember Australia?

A: My memories of Australian travel, are mixed up with trains transferring me, at unholy hours, from one too-exclusive State gauge to another; of enormous skies and primitive refreshment rooms, where I drank hot tea and ate mutton, while now and then a hot wind, like the look of the Punjab, boomed out of the emptiness. I went also to Sydney, which was populated by leisured multitudes all in their shirtsleeves and all picnicking all the day. (7)

Q: I'd love to hear you recite a poem. Would you mind reading "Cities, Thrones and Powers" – another favourite of mine.

A: Excellent choice!

CITIES THRONES AND POWERS

Cities and Thrones and Powers
Stand in Time's eye,
Almost as long as flowers,
Which daily die:
But as new buds put forth

To glad new men,
Out of the spent and unconsidered Earth
The Cities rise again.
This season's Daffodil,
She never hears
What change, what chance, what chill,
Cut down last year's;
But with bold countenance,
And knowledge small,
Esteems her seven days' continuance,
To be perpetual.
So, time that is o'er-kind
To all that be,
Ordains us e'en as blind,
As bold as she:
That in our very death,
And burial sure,
Shadow to shadow, well persuaded, saith,
"See how our works endure!" (8)

Q: How true! And speaking of time management, did you have a strict daily writing routine?

A: I worked rigorously every day from 9 a.m. to 1 p.m. at my desk. I was never disturbed, for to enter into my study one had to pass through a smaller room – it was called the dragon's chamber – where my wife sat with her knitting needles and with a sharp lookout against any unwelcome intruders. It was there that I wrote: "Captain Courageous" and the two Jungle Books. So, Mrs. Kipling's vigilance did not go un-rewarded. (9)

Q: I read somewhere, if you write at the exact same time and place every day – then your Muse will always know where and when to find you. Do you agree?

A: The magic of Literature lies in the words, and not in any man. Witness, a thousand excellent, strenuous words can leave us quite cold or put us to sleep, whereas a bare half-hundred words breathed upon by some man in his agony, or in his exaltation, or in his idleness, ten generations ago, can still lead whole nations into and out of captivity, can open to us the doors of the three worlds, or stir us so intolerably that we can scarcely abide to look at our own souls. It is a miracle—one that happens very seldom. But secretly each one of the masterless men with the words has hope, or has had hope, that the miracle may be wrought again through him. (10)

Q: What are your thoughts on the origin of Fiction?

A: Fiction began when some man invented a story about another man. It developed when another man told tales about a woman. This strenuous epoch begat the first school of destructive criticism, as well as the First Critic, who spent his short but vivid life in trying to explain that a man need not be a hen to judge the merits of an omelette. He died; but the question he raised is still at issue. It was inherited by the earliest writers from their unlettered ancestors, who also bequeathed to them the entire stock of primeval plots and situations—those fifty ultimate comedies and tragedies to which the Gods mercifully limit human action and suffering. Most of the Arts admit the truth that it is not expedient to tell everyone everything. Fiction recognises no such bar. There is no human emotion or mood, which it is forbidden to assault—there is no canon of reserve or pity that need be respected—in fiction. Why should there be? The man, after all, is not telling the truth. He is only writing fiction. While he writes it, his world will extract from it just so much of truth or pleasure as it requires for the moment. In time a little more, or much less, of the residue may be carried forward to the general account, and there, perhaps, diverted to ends of which the writer never dreamed. (11)

Q: There is a story about you giving away "The Jungle Book" manuscript to a member of your household. Is it true?

A: It was given as a present to a nurse who had devoutly cared for my first-born child. I advised her to take the script and someday if she was in need of money, she might be able to sell it at a handsome price.

Years later when she was in need, she sold it and lived well for the remainder of her life. (12)

Q: What a generous gesture. How did you feel about being courted by the "Ladies Home Journal"?

A: Not at all. Millions of readers enjoyed "The Jungle Book," and I received more offers from magazines than I was able to accept.

On one occasion, the editor of the "Ladies Home Journal", Edward W. Bok, requested that I write a story for his magazine. I disliked the magazine, and so requested an exorbitant fee for the story hoping to scare off the editor.

However, Mr. Bok agreed on the price, so I dashed off the story of "William the Conqueror", threw it into the mailbox and thought that was the end of the matter. But it wasn't.

A few days later I received a note from Mr. Bok, saying that the story was "excellent", but would I mind making a "minor yet necessary change in the copy?"

The story contained a reference to whiskey and champagne, which were two beverages that were taboo in the "Ladies Home Journal." Mr. Bok asked if I would "be gracious enough to substitute a couple of milder drinks."

I replied promptly with: No, Mr. Kipling would not be gracious enough. Either you take the whiskey, or you return the story.

In the end Mr. Bok published the story as I had penned it. Thus, I was the first man ever privileged to pour a glass of whiskey into the pages of the "Ladies Home Journal. (13)

Q: Have you any advice to impart to writers in the future?

A: Do your duty, live stoically, live cleanly, live cheerfully. (14)

Mr. Kipling disappeared instantaneously without even time for a nod or a good-bye.

If you haven't read Mr. Kipling's' works - then you are in for a real treat. Check these out for starters - and soon you'll be wanting more and more:

The Man Who Would Be King
The Naulahka - A story of West and East
The Jungle Book
Captains Courageous
The Day's Work
Kim
A Book of Words
Something of Myself
Departmental Ditties
A Child's Garden
A Legend of Truth
The Hour of the Angel
The Cat that Walked By Himself
A Pilgrim's Way.

Poi carukiren!
Cathy McGough
Your Interviewer of Legendary Writers From Beyond

Chapter Twelve

DICKENS AND TELETUBBY HILLS

Welcome my friends to this week's interview with one of the greatest writers in the history of the world: Mr. Charles Dickens. A hush goes over the crowd!

You are about to meet a man, who was able to write not one novel, not two novels, but THREE NOVELS in a single year! Mr. Dickens didn't stop there either! He also edited a magazine and wrote an operetta in his "spare time." (1) His Muse was sure busy!

I don't think anyone would disagree with me, if I pronounced Mr. Dickens as the winner in the category of Famous First Lines. While we await Mr. Dickens' arrival, let's see if you can identify the work this line comes from:

I am born. (2)

Do you know it? Perhaps you require a little hint? Here you go then:

Whether I shall turn out to be the hero of my own life, or whether that station will be held by anybody else, these pages must show. (3)

Have you guessed it? Yes, you're correct if you thought the line was taken from "David Copperfield" which was first published in 1869.

It is nearly time for Mr. Dickens to make his appearance and so I am making my way towards the place where our interview will be conducted. Here, Mr. Dickens and I will be surrounded by Australia's natural beauty: magnificent gum trees, the Cooks River, Tele-tubby-like hills, a park and an unoccupied soccer pitch.

Charles Dickens was born in Lanport, in the County of Hampshire, England on February 7 in 1812. As a child when his father found himself in financial difficulty Charles worked in a Blacking Factory while his family was placed in a Debtor's Prison in 1824. After a difficult childhood, he attended Wellington Academy in London where he received some education and later became a reporter.

Ah, here is Mr. Dickens now, walking in my direction across the empty soccer pitch.

He appeared somewhat in awe of his surroundings and as I watched him, I wondered where the devil Madame Delatour was. She wasn't making Mr. Dickens feel very welcome since she was nowhere in sight.

Realizing that he was totally on his own, I rose from the wooden bench and made my way to him. As we drew nearer and nearer to each other I noticed his rather odd appearance.

Not knowing where to look, I gazed into the distance where I spotted Madame, hiding behind a tree and sniggering. Sometimes she can be very rude!

Mr. Dickens reached out his hand to me and said:

A flower come to life – was the look I was trying for. How did I do? (4)

I considered his intention, taking in his appearance from top to toe. After all he had asked for my opinion. His fiery red hair, beard and moustache. His bright green waistcoat. His lavender trousers. His scarlet necktie. His beaming eyes. (5)

I assured him that indeed he had been successful, for the birds and bees never lie.

Pleased with himself then, he sewed his arm under mine, as we walked towards the park bench. Then Mr. Dickens asked:

How may I be of service to you dear lady?

Q: First of all, thank you for joining me today. Many writers believe you must experience things first-hand in order to write about them. Was "Oliver Twist" autobiographical?

A: My father was sent to debtor's prison for three months for a debt of 40 pounds. Because we were so poor, I was sent to a blacking factory at the age of twelve. That is where I met my "Fagin." It was located in an old, rotting building near Hungerford Stairs. I did not fit in there and without education knew that I had been condemned to the hopeless routine of a wage slaver. I was there for only five months, but as a child, I felt I would be there forever. (6)

Q: How do you look back at that period of your life?

A: It is wonderful to me how I could have been so easily cast away at such an age. It is wonderful to me, that, even after my descent into the poor little drudge I had been since we came to London, no one had compassion enough on me – a child of singular abilities, quick, eager, delicate, and soon hurt bodily or mentally – to suggest that something might have been spared, as certainly it might have been, to place me at any common school. (7)

Q: And so, you created a character with whom you could identify, while at the same time informing your readers?

A: I wanted it to be the story of things as they really are. "Oliver Twist" was a social document, an expose of the horrors of the poor and outlawed. I wished to show the terrifying conditions of the workhouse, caused by the Poor Law of 1834, a law designed to make relief so unattractive that only the most desperate would resort to it. The philosophy behind the Poor Law was that the indigent flocked to the workhouse because they enjoyed being there, an attitude, which was ridiculous.

Thus, I described it as such: a regular place of public entertainment...a tavern where there was nothing to pay; a public breakfast, dinner, tea, and supper all year round; a brick mortar Elysium. The new law made rations so meagre that the poor would starve more quickly in a workhouse than they did outside. The menu included: Three meals of thin gruel a day, with an onion twice a week, and half a roll, on Sundays. (8)

Q: How did you come to write "A Tale of Two Cities"?

A: When I was acting with my children and friends in Mr. Wilkie Collins' drama of "The Frozen Deep," I first conceived the main idea of that story. A strong desire was upon me at the time to embody it in my own person; and I traced out in my fancy, the state of mind of which it would necessitate the presentation to an observant spectator, with particular care and interest.

As the idea became familiar to me, it gradually shaped itself into its present form. Throughout its execution, it had complete possession of me; I verified what was suffered on the pages, as I had suffered it all myself. (9)

Q: "David Copperfield" is an enthralling novel from start to finish. How long did it take for you to write it?

A: It would concern the reader little, perhaps, to know how sorrowfully the pen is laid down at the close of a two-years' imaginative task; or how an Author feels as if he were dismissing some portion of himself into the shadowy world, when a crowd of the creatures of his brain are going from him forever. Yet, I had nothing else to tell; unless, indeed, I were to confess, that no one can ever believe the narrative, in the reading, more than I believed it in the writing. (10)

Q: Many have compared writing a novel to giving birth...Your two-years of hard labour certainly brought a memorable character into the world.

A: Of all my books, I like it the best. It will be easily believed I am a fond parent to every child of my fancy, and that no one can ever love that family as dearly as I love them. But, like many fond parents, I have in my heart of hearts a favourite child. And his name is David Copperfield. (11)

DAVID COPPERFIELD

Chapter 1

I am Born.

Whether I shall turn out to be the hero of my own life, or whether that station will be held by anybody else, these pages must show. To begin my life with the beginning of my life, I record that I was born (as I have been informed and believe) on a Friday, at twelve o'clock at night. It was remarked that the clock began to strike, and I began to cry, simultaneously.

In consideration of the day and hour of my birth, it was declared by the nurse, and by some sage women in the neighbourhood who had taken a lively interest in me several months before there was any possibility of our becoming personally acquainted, first, that I was destined to be unlucky in life; and secondly, that I was privileged to see ghosts and spirits; both these gifts inevitably attaching as they believed, to all unlucky infants of either gender, born towards the small hours on a Friday night. (12)

Q: Mr. Dickens, when you travelled to North America for the first time in 1842, what do you remember the most about the long journey?

A: On the third morning, I was awakened from my sleep by a dismal shriek from my wife, who demanded to know whether there was any danger. I opened my eyes and looked out of the bed.

The water-jug was plunging and leaping like a lively dolphin; all the smaller articles were afloat, except my shoes, which were stranded on a carpet-bag, high and dry, like a couple of coal-barges. Suddenly I saw them spring into the air, and behold the looking glass, which was nailed to the wall, was sticking fast upon the ceiling. At the same time, the door had entirely disappeared and a new one opened up on the floor. It was then that I began to comprehend that the stateroom was standing on its head. (13)

Q: You and your wife must have been petrified. As someone who gets seasick taking a ferry across Sydney Harbour, how did you travel?

A: Not sea-sick, be it understood, in the ordinary acceptation of the term; I wish I had been but in a form which I have never seen or heard described, though I have no doubt it is very common.

I lay there, all the day long, quite coolly and contentedly; with no sense of weariness, with no desire to get up, or get better, or take the air; with no curiosity, or care, or regret, of any sort or degree, saving that I think I can remember, in this universal indifference, having a kind of lazy joy – a fiendish delight, if anything so lethargic can be dignified with the title – in the fact of my wife being too ill to talk to me. (14)

Q: Was travel by rail any better?

A: For miles and miles and miles we went on in deep solitudes, unbroken by any sign of human life or trace of human footstep; nor was anything seen to move about them but the blue jay, whose colour was so bright, and yet so delicate, that it looked like a flying flower. (15)

Q: Oh yes, the blue jay. What a perfect picture you have painted. Would you mind sharing your memories of one of the most beautiful places in the world, Niagara Falls?

A: When I drew near it on the ferry, then, is when I felt how near to my Creator I was standing, the first effect and the enduring one – instant and lasting – of the tremendous spectacle, was Peace, and Peace of Mind: Tranquillity: Calm recollections of the dead: Great thoughts of Eternal Rest and Happiness: nothing of Gloom and Terror. Niagara was at once stamped upon my heart, an Image of Beauty; to remain there, changeless and indelible, until its pulses cease to beat, forever.

Oh, how the strife and trouble of our daily life receded from my view, and lessened in the distance, during the ten memorable days we passed on that Enchanted Ground!

What voices spoke from out the thundering water what faces, faded from the earth, looked out upon me from its gleaming depths what Heavenly promise glistened in those angels' tears, the drops of many hues, that showered around, and twined themselves about the gorgeous arches which the changing rainbow's made!

To wander to and fro all day, and see the cataracts from all points of view; to stand upon the edge of the great Horse Shoe Falls, marking the hurried water gathering strength as it approached the verge, yet seeming, too, to pause before it shot into the gulf below; to gaze from the river's level up at the torrent as it came streaming down; to climb the neighbouring heights and watch it through the trees, and see the wreathing water in the rapids hurrying on to take its fearful plunge; to linger in the shadow of the solemn rocks three miles below; watching the river as, stirred by no visible cause, it heaved and eddied and awoke the echoes, being troubled yet far down beneath the surface, by its giant leap; to have Niagara before me, lighted by the sun and by the moon, red in the day's decline, and grey as evening slowly fell upon it; to look upon it every day, and wake up in the night and hear its ceaseless voice: this was enough. (16)

Q: What a trip back home Mr. Dickens. Thank you! Do you have any advice for writers in 2003 and beyond?

A: I would simply say that I believe no true man, with anything to tell, need have the least misgiving, either for himself or his message, before a large number of hearers – always supposing that he be not afflicted with the coxcombical idea of writing down to the popular intelligence, instead of writing the popular intelligence up to himself, if perchance, he be above it; - and, provided always that he deliver himself plainly of what is in him, which seems to be no unreasonable stipulation, it being supposed that he has some dim design of making himself understood. (17)

Q: I'm afraid our time is coming to an end. Will you recite a poem for me? Should you begin to fade, I will finish it for you.

When Mr. Dickens commenced reading, children appeared one by one, from beyond the Tele-tubby-like hills. At first, they giggled at the funny man, dressed like a flower and he gave them a wink. They gathered around him and listened intently:

A: This poem is for all of you little ones, come closer, I don't bite.

He smiled as the children drew nearer and waited until they were all quietly seated, then he began:

THE CHILDREN

When the lessons all are ended,
And the school for the day is dismissed,
And the little ones gather round me
To bid me good-night and be kissed;
Oh! The little white arms that encircle
My neck in a tender embrace!
Oh! The smiles that are halos of Heaven
Shedding sunshine of joy on my face!
And when they are gone I sit dreaming
Of my childhood, too lovely to last;
Of love that my heart well remembers
When it wakes to the pulse of the past,
Ere the world and its wickedness made me
A portion of sorrow and sin –

When the glory of God was about me,
And the glory of gladness within.
Oh! My heart grows as weak as a woman's
And the fountain of feeling will flow
When I think of the path, steep and stony,
Where the feet of the dear ones must go;
Of the mountains of sin hanging o'er them.
Of the tempest of fate blowing wild;
Oh! There's nothing on earth half so holy
As the innocent heart of a child.
They are idols of hearts and of households;
They are angels of God, in disguise;
His sunlight still sleeps in their tresses,
His glory still gleams in their eyes.
Oh! Those truants from home and from Heaven.
They make me more manly and mild;
And I know now how Jesus can liken
The kingdom of God to a child.
I ask not a life for the dear ones,
All radiant, as others have done;
But that life may have just enough shadow
To temper the glare of the sun.
I would pray God to guard them from evil –
But my prayer would bound back to myself –
A seraph can pray for a sinner,
But a sinner must pray for himself.
The twig is so easily bended,
I have banished the rule and the rod;
I have taught them the goodness of knowledge,
They have taught me the goodness of God.
My heart is a dungeon of darkness;
When I shut them from breaking a rule;
My frown is sufficient correction –
My love is the law of the school.
I shall leave the old house in the autumn

To traverse its threshold no more.
Ah! How I shall sigh for the dear ones
That meet me each morn at the door!
I shall miss the "good-nights" and the kisses,
And the gush of their innocent glee,
The group on the green, and the flowers
That are brought every morning to me.

In anticipation of Mr. Dickens' imminent departure, Madame Delatour whisked him away. I continued reading:

I shall miss them at morn and at even,
Their songs in the school and the street;
I shall miss the low hum of their voices,
And the tramp of their delicate feet
When the lessons and tasks are all ended,
And death says, "The school is dismissed,"
May the little ones gather around me
To bid me goodnight and be kissed. (18)

The children and parents applauded simultaneously. I bowed and proceeded to make my way towards home.

A part of my heart felt unsettled as I strolled along my usual path, winding around Cooks River. Waves jumped up, seemingly trying to catch my attention. I saw them, lapping upon the shores but ignored their performance. My heart was pining for Niagara. And today, nothing could still that longing.

The following novels will leave you wanting more:

Oliver Twist
Nicholas Nickleby
The Old Curiosity Shop
A Christmas Carol
David Copperfield
A Tale of Two Cities
Great Expectations
American Notes For General Circulation
The Song of the Wreck

A School Boy's Story
Nobody Story
A Child's Story.

Cheerio!
Cathy McGough
Your Interviewer of Legendary Writers From Beyond

Chapter Thirteen

DOSTOEVSKY AT HEATHROW

I can well remember that day almost like it was yesterday. We were at Heathrow Airport, awaiting our flight. The airline had cancelled it, delayed it – and they didn't seem to have any idea when we'd be on our way.

Madame Delatour and I had been in London for twelve days. May in England meant rain and more rain. Good for the flowers, but not so good for tourists. One place we visited meant more to us because of the rain.

My mind wandered back to John Fowles' hometown "Lyme Regis." There, I walked along "The Cobb" – in the footsteps of Fowles' Sarah Woodruff from "The French Lieutenant's Woman." The rain soaked me to the skin as the wind forced me out further and further along the narrow stony harbour wall. Out to where I felt vulnerable to the elements - unprotected – like the wind was willing the sleeves of my jacket to take flight.

Jolted back to reality by a voice on the loudspeaker, I looked around the crowded waiting room for Blanchetta. It seemed like she had disappeared. I checked out the gift shops, toilets and everywhere else I could think of but couldn't find her. Since there was still no word on our departure, I laid down for another nap.

Hours later, the clip-clip-clipping of high heels echoing along the corridors awoke me with a startle. Someone was calling my name. I wiped the sleep from my eyes as Blanchetta swooped upon me. She was so excited no words came out of her mouth although her tongue was wagging.

Apparently, she had fallen asleep, and Russian writer Fyodor Dostoevsky had contacted her. He asked if it would be possible to return to the year 2001 and do an interview. Blanchetta was clearly enthusiastic about Mr. Dostoevsky.

At first, I wasn't sure about the location. I looked around me, seeing passengers coming and going, to-ing and fro-ing, and wondered if anyone would recognize our guest if he just popped in.

After some consideration, we decided it was too risky to bring Mr. Dostoevsky back to earth in such chaos. Disgruntled travellers were lounging everywhere, restless children, and impatient parents - there were way too many distractions to give Mr. Dostoevsky the attention he deserved.

In the end, we requested a room for a business meeting - which the airline graciously provided. (At least they got one thing right!)

Fyodor Dostoevsky was born on October 30, in 1821, in Varvara, Russia. To say that Mr. Dostoevsky had a difficult life is the understatement of all time. By 1866, when his most famous novel "Crime and Punishment" was published he had already written "Poor Folk", "The Double", "Notes from the Dead House", and "Notes from Underground." In January 1879, his last novel, "The Brothers Karamazov" sold 1,500 copies in a few days. (1) Two years later, he died in extreme poverty leaving nothing "except his books." (2)

Pulling out my copy I began reading:

NOTES FROM UNDERGROUND

It was not only that I could not become spiteful, I did not know how to become anything: neither spiteful nor kind, neither a rascal nor an honest man, neither a hero nor an insect.

Mr. Dostoevsky entered. Seeing I was reading his book he motioned to take it. I handed it to him, with my page marker. I was delighted when began reading his work to me.

Now, I am living out my life in my corner, taunting myself with the spiteful and useless consolation that an intelligent man cannot become anything seriously, and it is only the fool who becomes anything. Yes, a man in the nineteenth century must and morally ought to be pre-eminently a characterless creature; a man of character, an active man, is pre-eminently a limited creature. That is my conviction of forty years. I am forty years old now, and you know forty years is a whole lifetime; you know it is extreme old age. To live longer than forty years be bad manners, is vulgar, immoral. I will tell you who do fools and worthless fellows. I tell all old men that to their faces, all these venerable old men, all these silver-haired and reverend seniors! I tell the whole world that to its face. I have a right to say so, for I shall go on living to sixty myself. To seventy! To eighty! (3)

I had been observing Mr. Dostoevsky's performance. Of particular interest was the way his copper-haired beard fit into the open space of the jacket of his brown suit totally obliterating the shirt he wore underneath. His eyes were full of laughter while he read, but when he finished the laughter disappeared to reveal a deep sadness. He regained his composure, smiled and walked towards us. He thanked Madame Delatour and me for giving him the opportunity to return to London in the year 2001.

The vault in my mind went click. I recalled reading somewhere about Mr. Dostoevsky's visit to London's World Fair at the Crystal Palace in 1862. (4)

Q: Mr. Dostoevsky, will you tell me about your first visit to London?

A: The World Fair was truly magnificent. You felt the tremendous power which had attracted there that mass of people from all over the world into one herd...And no matter how free and independent you might have felt before; there you were seized with an unknown fear...

There was something biblical about the scene, something Babylonian, as if the prophecy from the Apocalypse had come true. You became suddenly aware that it would take much spiritual resistance and denial over centuries to withstand the pressure and not to succumb completely to the awesome impression, not to bow to the fact and not to worship Mammon, in other words, not to accept the existing for the ideal... (5)

Madame Delatour returned to the room carrying some refreshments. Mr. Dostoevsky immediately spied the pot of steaming hot tea and accepted a cup. Then he asked Madame Delatour if she would be kind enough to purchase some tobacco so that he could roll a cigarette. (6)

Not wanting to scold him on the bad effects of smoking (since he was already deceased) Madame Delatour brought him the necessaries. He unexpectedly asked:

Q: Might I have a penholder? (7)

Neither of us had one, but I passed over my Parker Pen and watched as Mr. Dostoevsky rolled the cigarette and then placed it between his lips.

Realising there were no matches on hand, Madame Delatour made the motion to leave the room and purchase some, but Mr. Dostoevsky explained it wasn't necessary. He suggested we continue with the interview since our time was limited.

Q: Did you always love reading, even when you were a lad?

A: My brothers and sisters and I (including myself we numbered seven) revelled in Walter Scott and "The Arabian Nights" and we had profound knowledge of "Robinson Crusoe." When we passed the summer months on our father's country estate at Darovoye, which was two days drive from Moscow. We liked to pretend we were on a desert island or else we were Red Indians from the pages of "The Last Mohicans." (8)

Q: You were imprisoned in Siberia and put to work doing hard labour for four years. What was the worst thing you remember about being in prison?

A: To be alone, is a necessity of normal existence, like eating or drinking; otherwise in that forced communal life you become a hater of mankind. The society of people acts like a poison or an infection. There were moments when I hated everyone who crossed my path, whether they were blameless or guilty and I regarded them as thieves who were stealing my life with impunity. (9)

It occurred to me that if it were desired to reduce a man to nothing – to punish him atrociously so that even the most hardened murderer would tremble before the punishment, it would only be necessary to give his work a character of complete uselessness and absurdity. (10)

Q: Were you given books to pass the time?

A: Officially I was only allowed to read "The Bible", but during the last months a kindly doctor in the hospital slipped into my hands translations of "The Pickwick Papers" and "David Copperfield." As soon as I was free, I wrote to my brother begging for books, books and still more books. (11)

Q: I am in the process of writing my first novel, is there any advice you can offer to me?

A: This is what I knew for certain when I began writing "The Insulted and Injured", my first novel, at the time: 1) that even though the novel should be a failure, there would be poetry in it; 2) that there would be two or three burning and powerful passages in it; 3) that the two most important characters would be portrayed truthfully and even artistically. This certainly was enough for me. The resulting work was weird, but there are some fifty pages in it of which I am proud... (12)

Q: Having read "The Insulted and Injured" I can vouch firsthand that there is much more for you to be proud of in it. Could I persuade you to read a passage from that book?

Mr. Dostoevsky reached into the pocket of his jacket and pulled out his glasses. He never wore them in public, only in private and I felt privileged he felt comfortable enough to don them in my presence. (13)

A: I would prefer to read you a little something from this book instead:

THE DEVILS

There was a waterfall there, a very small one; it fell from high up in the mountains, like a thin thread, all white and foaming. It fell from a great height, but seemed to be very near, and it was half a mile away, but you would have said it was only fifty yards. I loved to listen to the sound at night, and at such moments I would become terribly restless. Sometimes at noon I would walk in the mountains and stand there, half-way up the mountainside with the old resinous pines around me, so tall they were, and somewhere high up on the precipitous cliffs there was a medieval castle in ruins, far away, and the little village lay below, far away, almost invisible, and the sun shone, and the sky was so blue and there was only this terrible silence all around me. I thought I heard a mysterious summons, and then it would come to me that if I went straight on and continued to walk for a long while, I would come to the line where earth and sky meet, and then I would find the key to the whole mystery and discover a new form of life richer and more splendid than ours. I dreamed of a great city as large as Naples full of palaces and tumult and exciting life, and then it struck me that life can be enjoyed just as magnificently in prison. (14)

Q: Did readers find your work to be too raw, too realistic?

A: Reality is not limited to what we are familiar with. For it contains an enormous portion of something in the form of the unsaid future Word. I have my own view of reality and what most people call fantastic and exceptional is to me the very essence of the real. The commonplace side of events and conventional views on them are not yet realism, but rather it's opposite. One's portrayal of things is far weaker than the things themselves...My views about reality and realism differ from those of our realists and critics...Their realism is incapable of explaining a fraction of real, actual facts, but we even attempt to prophecy facts all of the time. Duplicity masks the other side of the truth – all this is bad enough. But if all people should come forth now as they really are, then I say to you it would be much worse. They call me a psychologist. That is not correct. I am a realist in the full sense of the word, that is, I try to portray the depths of the human soul...As a realist I seek the human being in man. (15)

Q: Is it true that you burned an almost finished draft of Crime and Punishment?"

A: I sat over my work like a prisoner. It was a novel for the "Russian Messenger." It was a long novel in six parts. Towards the end of November 1865, a lot was written and finished. I burned it all. I did not like it myself. A new form, a new plan carried me away and I started afresh. I worked day and night and still I worked too little. The novel is a poetic thing, it demands calm of mind and of imagination. At the time my creditors were tormenting me, threatening to send me to jail. (16)

Q: Is it true you nearly lost the copyrights to your work?

A: I foolishly sold all the copyrights to a profiteering publisher in order to meet my debts. If I didn't write a new novel by Nov. 1, 1866, all of my works, including works, which I had yet to write, were to become the property of that publisher. I began "Crime and Punishment" and in November burned it. In twenty-six days, I wrote more than 200 pages, which became "The Gambler" and successfully met the deadline and paid my debts. (17)

Discussing these matters seemed to agitate Mr. Dostoevsky who was rolling up cigarette after cigarette. He looked around, cagey as a rabbit – until Madame Delatour reached over and lit his cigarette for him.

I am convinced that not one of our other writers, past or present, dead, or alive, wrote under such conditions as those under which I had to write all of the time. Some like Turgenev would have died at the mere thought. If they only knew how depressing it was to ruin an idea, which was born in you, about which you became enthusiastic, about which you knew that it was good – and to be forced to ruin it knowingly! (18)

His heartfelt words brought tears to my eyes, and I took his trembling hands into mine and began to recite his own words to him. In fact, the exact same words for which he had been given a standing ovation during his speech before the "Society of friends of Russian Literature" in August 1880. This speech was later recorded in "The Diary of a Writer" -

Humble thyself, proud man! Above all, break down thy haughtiness! Humble thyself, ye idlers, and learn to labour in our sacred earth!

Truth is within thee; it is not to be found without. Therefore, find thyself within! It is not thy task to overwhelm others. Subdue thyself! Be master of thyself! Thus, shalt though perceive truth!

Not in things, nor without thee, nor in distant lands lies the truth. It lies in thine own seeking for self-improvement. If thou conquerest thyself, if thou humblest thyself, then shalt thou be free beyond thy dreams. Thou shalt labour at a worthy task. Thou shalt make others free, and therein shall thou find happiness, since thy life will be fulfilled, and thou shalt discover at last an understanding of thine own people and their sacred truth. (19)

His eyes filled with compassion, and tears flowed down his hollowed cheeks as his image started to fade in and out. He did not regret returning to earth. He never contemplated it would be such a painful resurrection.

I felt to blame for bringing memories flooding back into his mind. It had not been my intention. Mr. Dostoevsky read my thoughts and gently patted the back of my hand in a fatherly way as he disappeared from Heathrow Airport, now and forever.

As I sat, looking at his vacant chair, I couldn't help but remember the following words from:

THE MEEK

"Why did she die?" he cries, "...O we could have solved everything...Why, why couldn't we come together again and start a new life? Only a few words, two days, no more, and she would have understood everything...What hurts most is that all this is an accident, a simply barbarous, stupid accident! That's what hurts. Five minutes, just late!!!... "People, love one another" – who said that? Who said we must love one another? How unfeelingly the clock ticks on. It's now two o'clock in the morning. Her shoes lie there by the bed as if they are waiting for her...No, really, when they've carried her out tomorrow, what will become of me?" (20)

I closed the book, picked up my suitcase and lost myself in a crowd. My heart was heavy and when I was finally on my way back home, I slept a dreamless sleep.

You cannot go wrong when reading any of Fyodor Dostoevsky's Novels. Be patient and your rewards will be many!

Poor Folk
The Gambler
The Idiot
The Insulted and Injured
The Devils
The Brothers Karamazov
The Eternal Husband

The Meek
Notes from Underground
Crime and Punishment
The Double
A Raw Youth
The House of the Dead
The Diary of a Writer
Gentle Spirit
Crocodile
The Dream of a Ridiculous Man
Little Orphan
The Landlady
The Stranger-Woman
A Christmas Tree and a Wedding
An Honest Thief.

Do svidaniya!
Cathy McGough
Your Interviewer of Legendary Writers From Beyond

Chapter Fourteen

KEATS VISITS MY BIRTHPLACE

It was on a sunny day in the early autumn of 1999, while sitting on the banks of the Avon River, in my birthplace of Stratford (Ontario, Canada), that an unexpected guest made an appearance.

I had scattered a blanket across the freshly mowed grass, and the scent was wafting ever so lightly through the blanket. The glorious swans were moving towards me making their voices heard in hope of a crust of bread.

The blue jays and robins were twittering, and the setting was perfect for a John Keats' poem:

TO AUTUMN
Season of mists and mellow fruitfulness,
Close bosom-friend of the maturing sun;
Conspiring with him how to load and bless
With fruit the vines that round the thatch eaves run;
To bend with apples, the mossed cottage-trees,
And fill all fruit with ripeness to the core;
To swell the gourd, and plump the hazel shells

With a sweet kernel; to set budding more,
And still more, later flowers for the bees,
Until they think warm days will never cease,
For Summer has o'er-brimmed their clammy cells.
Who hath not seen there oft amid thy store?
Sometimes whoever seeks abroad may find
Thee sitting careless on a granary floor,
Thy hair soft-lifted by the winnowing wind;
Or on a half-reaped furrow sound asleep,
Drowsed with the fume of poppies, while thy hook
Spares the next swath and all its twined flowers:
And sometime like a gleaner thou dost keep
Steady thy laden head across a brook;
Or by a cider-press, with patient look,
Thou watchest the last oozings, hours by hours.
Where are the songs of Spring? Ay, where are they?
Think not of them, thou hast thy music too, -
While barred clouds bloom the soft dying day,
And touch the stubble-plains with rosy hue;
Then in a wailful choir the small gnats mourn
Among the rivers sallows, borne aloft
Or sinking as the light wind lives or dies;
And full-grown lambs bleat from hilly bourn,
Hedge-crickets sing; and now with treble soft
The redbreast whistles from a garden-croft,
And gathering swallows twitter in the skies. (1)

I awoke with a startle, caused by the rumbling engine of a throaty sounding Trans Am and looked around anxiously, for I had been expecting Madame Delatour. At first, I could not see her and then I heard footsteps on the Island Bridge and noticed she was leading John Keats towards me.

John Keats was born prematurely on either the 29th or 31st of October in 1795, in a stable at the sign of the Swan and Hoop, Finsbury Pavement - facing the then open space of

Lower Moorfield. (2) He was not long for this world and died at the tender age of 25 on February 23, 1821.

Slowly he walked towards me, while his boots made a clank, clank, clanking sound when they kissed the wooden bridge.

John Keats wore a dark suit, with many silver buttons on the front as well as along the cuffs. Inside was a white shirt with a matching cravat. His most distinguishing characteristics were his red curly hair and his dreamy blue eyes. He glanced about from side to side like a child in a candy store.

He took my hand into his, asking what enchanted place he had been invited to visit. In particular, he was interested in the large glass atrium-like building, which was framed by the beauty behind us.

I explained that the building was "The Stratford Festival" - an idea conceived by Tom Patterson in the 1950s devoted to live performances of plays, and in specific the works of William Shakespeare.

I never quite despair when I read Shakespeare - indeed I shall I think never read any other Book much. Now this might lead me into a long Confab, but I desist. I am very near agreeing with Hazlitt that Shakespeare is enough for us. (3)

Q: Someone once said, "Variety is the spice of life" – Shakespeare yes, but some Keats is also necessary. Would you mind sharing your earliest childhood memory?

A: First, please call me John - and thank you for your kind words. Although I cannot remember why I did it, I do recall grabbing a sword, then standing in the door of my mother's bedroom announcing, "no one must enter or leave this house!" I was but 5 at the time and believe we had company. I lived life with my entire being and "could feel joy and sorrow with my hands." (4)

Q: Is there a time you can remember – when you decided a poet's life was for you?

A: My dear parents both died before I turned 15, my years with them I fondly compared to the reading of an ever-changing tale came to a halt. My guardian apprenticed me to a surgeon in Edmonton (near London.) I wrote to my friends desperately requesting a copy of Spenser's "Faery Queen" and read the scenes like a young colt turned loose in a spring meadow. That was when I first caught the poet's fever. (5)

Q: Did you have a regular routine for writing?

A: I read and wrote about eight hours a day. There is an old saying "well begun is half done" - 'tis a bad one. I would use instead, "Not begun at all till half done;" so according to that I have not begun my Poem and consequently (a priori) can say nothing about it. Thank God! (6)

Q: Did you believe you would be regarded as a great poet one day?

A: There is no greater Sin after the seven deadly than to flatter oneself into an idea of being a great Poet - or one of those beings who are privileged to wear out their Lives in the pursuit of Honour - how comfortable a feel it is that such a Crime must bring its heavy Penalty? That if one be a Self-deluder account will be balanced? (7)

Q: What part did imagination play in your writing?

A: I am certain of nothing but of the holiness of the heart's affections, and the truth of imagination. What the imagination seizes as beauty must be truth - whether it existed before or not, - for I have the same idea of all our passions as of love: they are all, in their sublime, creative of essential beauty. In a word, you may know my favourite speculation by my first book, and the little song I send in my last, which is a representation from the fancy of the probable mode of operating in these matters. The imagination may be compared to Adam's dream - he awoke and found it truth. I am more zealous in this affair because I have never yet been able to perceive how anything can be known for truth by consecutive reasoning - and yet it must be. The simple imaginative mind may have its rewards in the repetition of its own silent working coming continually on the spirit with a fine suddenness. (8)

Q: Do you believe that earthly happiness is achievable?

A: I scarcely remember counting upon any happiness - I look for it if it be not in the present hour, - nothing startles me beyond the moment. The setting sun will always set me to rights, or if a sparrow come before my window, I take part in its existence and pick about the gravel. The first thing that strikes me on hearing a misfortune having befallen another is this - 'Well, it cannot be helped: he will have the pleasure of trying the resources of his spirit.' (9)

Q: Do you regret never having married?

A: I hoped I would never marry. Though the most beautiful Creatures were waiting for me at the end of a Journey or a Walk; though the Carpet were of Silk, the Curtains of the morning Clouds; the chairs and Sofa stuffed with Cygnet's down; the food Manna, the Wine beyond Claret, the Window opening on Winander Mere, I should not feel - or rather my Happiness would not be so fine, as my Solitude is sublime.

Then instead of what I have described, there is a sublimity to welcome me home - The roaring of the wind is my wife and the Stars through the windowpane are my Children. The mighty abstract Idea I have of Beauty in all things stifles the more divided and minute domestic happiness - an amiable wife and sweet Children I contemplate as a part of that Beauty, but I must have a thousand of those beautiful particles to fill up my heart.

I felt more and more every day, as my imagination strengthened, that I did not live in the world alone but in a thousand worlds - No sooner was I alone than shapes of epic greatness were stationed around me, and served my Spirit the office which was equivalent to a King's bodyguard - then “Tragedy with sceptred pall came sweeping by.” According to my state of mind I was with Achilles shouting in the Trenches or with Theocritus in the Vales of Sicily. Or I would throw my whole being into Troilus, and repeating those lines, "I wander like a lost Soul upon the Stygian Banks staying for waftage," I melt into the air with voluptuousness so delicate that I was content to be alone. These things, combined with the opinion I have of the generality of women - who appear to me as children to whom I would rather give a sugar plum than my time, form a barrier against Matrimony which I rejoice in. (10)

Q: A sugarplum! Perhaps it is a good thing you never married then. Do you believe it is necessary to experience something firsthand in order to write about it?

A: Nothing ever becomes real till it is experienced - Even a Proverb is no proverb to you till your Life hast illustrated it. I compared human life to a large Mansion of many apartments, two of which I can only describe, the doors of the rest being as yet shut upon me. The first we step into we call the Infant, or Thoughtless Chamber, in which we remain if we do not think.

We remain there a long while, and notwithstanding the doors of the second Chamber remain as open, showing a bright appearance, we care not to hasten to it; but are at length imperceptibly impelled by the awakening of the thinking principle within us – we no sooner get into the second Chamber, which I shall call the Chamber of Maiden Thought, than we become intoxicated with the light and the atmosphere, we see nothing but pleasant wonders, and think of delaying there for ever in delight.

However, among the affects this breathing is father of, is that tremendous one of sharpening one's vision into the heart and nature of Man – of convincing one's nerves that the world is full of misery and heartbreak, pain, sickness and oppression – whereby this Chamber of Maiden Thought becomes gradually darkened and at the same time on all sides of it, many doors are set to open – but all dark – all leading to dark passages. We see not the balance of the good and evil; we are in a mist, we are now in that state, we feel the "Burden of Mystery." Now if we live, and go on thinking, we shall explore all of the passages. (11)

Q: Did you care what others thought of you?

A: Some thought me middling, others silly, others foolish - everyone thought he saw my weak side against my will, when in truth it is with my will - I was content to be thought all this because I have in my own breast so great a resource.

This was one great reason why they liked me so: because they could all show to advantage in a room and eclipse from a certain tact one who is reckoned to be a good Poet.

I hoped I was not here playing tricks "to make the angels weep." I thought not: for I had not the least contempt for my species, and though it may sound paradoxical, my greatest elevations of soul left me every time more humbled - Enough of this - though in your Love for me you will not think it enough. (12)

Q: You are right; I enjoy listening to you and wish we had more time. Could you describe how you saw the world?

A: I hated the world: it battered too much the wings of my self-will, and would I could have taken a sweet poison from your lips to send me out of it. From no others would I take it. (13)

I was taken aback by his statement and blushed furiously.

Q: In twenty-five years, you achieved more than many writers do in their lifetime. Was immortality your driving force?

A: I have left no immortal work behind me - nothing to make my friends proud of my memory - but I have loved the principle of beauty in all things, and if I had had time, I would have made myself remembered. (14)

Q: What advice do you have for Poets in the future?

A: First, I think poetry should surprise by a fine excess, and not by singularity; it should strike the reader as a wording of his own highest thoughts and appear almost a remembrance.

Second, its touches of beauty should never be halfway, thereby making the reader breathless, instead of content. The rise, the progress, the setting of Imagery, should, like the sun, come natural to him, shine over him, and set soberly, although in magnificence, leaving him in the luxury of twilight.

But it is easier to think what poetry should be, than to write it. And this leads me to another point.

Third, if poetry comes not as naturally as the leaves to a tree, it had better not come at all. (15)

Q: John, you are one of the most revered poets of all time, honoured at Westminster Abbey in the Poet's Corner and schools all over the world study your poetry every year. Do you feel your success relied more on circumstances?

A: Circumstances are like Clouds continually gathering and bursting - While we are laughing the seed of some trouble is put into the wide arable land of events - while we are laughing it sprouts, it grows and suddenly bears a poison fruit, which we must pluck. (16)

Q: What is your definition of a Poet?

A: A Poet is the most un-poetical of any thing in existence; because he has no Identity - he is continually in for - and filling some other Body - The Sun, the Moon, the Sea and Men and Women who are creatures of impulse are poetical and have about them an unchangeable attribute - the poet has none; no identity - he is certainly the most un-poetical of all God's Creatures. (17)

Q: I am a Poet, and my Muse has abandoned me. Is there any advice you can give to me – to get back to writing again?

A: Don't be discouraged by a failure. It can be a positive experience. Failure is, in a sense, the highway to success, inasmuch as every discovery of what is false leads us to seek earnestly after what is true, and every fresh experience points out some form of error, which we shall afterwards carefully avoid.

Poetry should please by a fine excess and not by singularity. It should strike the reader as a wording of his own highest thoughts and appear almost as a remembrance. (18)

Q: Your friend Lord Byron, is quoted as saying that the review in "The Quarterly" may have taken you to an early death is that true?

A: It did me not the least harm in society to make me appear little and ridiculous: I know when a man is superior to me and give him all due respect - he would be the last to laugh at me and as for the rest I felt that I made an impression upon them which insured me personal respect while I was in sight whatever they may have said when my back was turned.

The only thing that can ever affect me personally for more than one short passing day, is any doubt about my powers for poetry - I seldom have any, and I look with hope to the nighing time when I shall have none. I am as happy as a Man can be. (19)

Q: Would you please read one of your poems?

A: Let me think. Yes, I know just the one:

THE HUMAN SEASONS

Four seasons fill the measure of the year;
There are four seasons in the mind of man;
He has his lusty Spring, when fancy clear
Takes in all beauty with an easy span:
He has his Summer, when luxuriously
Spring's honey'd cud of youthful thought he loves
To ruminate, and by such dreaming high
Is nearest unto heaven: quiet coves
His soul has in its Autumn, when his wings
He furleth close; contented so to look
On mists in idleness – to let fair things

Pass by unheeded as a threshold brook.
He has his Winter too of pale misfeature,
Or else he would forego his mortal nature. (20)

While John was reading, a group of young girls dressed in school uniforms began to gather around him. When he finished, they applauded, giggling, and whispering as the boldest of the group moved forward and asked him for his autograph.

John was taken aback by all the attention, but at the same time incredibly pleased. He asked each of the girls their names and signed his name for them.

The girls whispered among themselves and then bid us farewell as they went on their way. They hadn't gone very far, when I noticed John was beginning to fade in and out. I barely had the opportunity to wave good-bye before he disappeared.

As they were walking away, I heard one of the girls read his name aloud and say:

"John Keats? I wonder which play he's in. He sure is cute!"

I rolled up my blanket and walked away from the flowing Avon River, hoping that one day those girls would read and discover the works of John Keats. I had a feeling the autograph they received might be "Writ in water" like the words which were recorded upon his tombstone.

I leave you now with the following words:

"Bards of passion and of mirth, who have left your souls on earth. You have souls in Heaven too, double-lived in regions new." (21)

Find out more about John Keats by reading the inspiring collection he has left behind. I encourage you to seek out the following:

The Eve of St. Agnes
The Eve of St. Mark
Hyperion
Endymion

Lamia
Sleep and Poetry
To a Nightingale
On a Grecian Urn
To Psyche
On Melancholy
Bards of Passion and of Mirth
When I Have Fears
On First Looking into Chapman's Homer
The Grasshopper and Cricket
On Seeing a Lock of Milton's Hair
The Human Seasons
To Byron
Where's The Poet.

Wes du hal!
Cathy McGough
Your Interviewer of Legendary Writers From Beyond

Chapter Fifteen

HENRY WADSWORTH LONGFELLOW MEMENTOES

It is dusk and very soon our guest will be arriving. This evening Madame Delatour will be contacting Henry Wadsworth Longfellow who has been proclaimed America's finest Poet of all time.

We are contacting him in the evening, so we can enjoy one of our favourite pastimes together - walking. With any luck the path will be relatively clear from joggers, bicyclers and the like so that Mr. Longfellow and I can walk in peace.

Henry Wadsworth Longfellow was born on February 27, 1807 in Portland, Oregon. Mr. Longfellow was a poet, who lived his life to the words "the pen is mightier than the sword." He never shied away from conflict and always fought for the rights of his fellow citizens. In essence, his soul nurtured the wilderness of America. (1)

Madame Delatour was busy contacting Mr. Longfellow, and in the meantime, I read aloud an untitled poem which I recently discovered in a book called "Borrowings." Its suede covers flapped with time and rightly so since the date of publication was 1899. Although far from being in perfect condition, I knew instantly that it had been battered and tattered with love. Inside, there were many newspaper clippings of poems.

Within its treasures the book contained this untitled gem, which is credited to Mr. Longfellow:

As a tired mother when the day is o'er,
Leads by the hand her little child to bed,
Half willing, half reluctant to be led,
And leaves his broken playthings on the floor,
Still gazing at them through the open door,
Nor wholly reassured and comforted
By promises of others in their stead,
Which though more splendid, may not please him more
So nature deals with us and takes away
Our playthings one by one, and by the hand
Leads us to rest so gently that we go
Scarce knowing if we wish to go or stay,
Being too full of sleep to understand
How far the unknown transcends the what we know. (2)

I gently closed the book, taking care all its odds and bods remained inside, when noticed Henry Wadsworth Longfellow walking towards me on the path.

He was of medium height, with a head and face, which were eminently poetic. The great charm of his face centred in his eyes of unclouded blue, deep-set, under overhanging brows, which held an indescribable expression of thought and tenderness. Though seamed with many wrinkles, his face had a rosy hue of health and his hair was snow-white. His manner had a child's simplicity yet was of an impregnable dignity. (3)

He introduced himself and extended his hand. I was abashed at his quiet and humble manner and immediately felt like he was an old friend, returning from a long journey. We walked, arm in arm as I looked into his blue eyes and began our interview.

Q: When you were a child, you loved to read. What books made the greatest impression upon your young mind?

A: I was very fortunate as a child, to have a full Library of books to entertain me. My father saw to that, although he did not want me to become a writer. Writers who I adored were Shakespeare, Milton, and Pope, Dryden and Goldsmith, to name but a few. I loved "The Arabian Nights" and "Don Quixote" ... but the first book to fascinate my imagination was Washington Irving's "Sketch Book." I read it with "ever increasing wonder and delight, spell-bound by its pleasant humour, its melancholy tenderness, its atmosphere of reverie – nay, even by its grey-brown covers, the shaded letters of its titles, and the fair, clear type, which seemed an outward symbol of its style. (4)

Q: Your father did not want you to become a writer?

A: When I was at college, I made up my mind to embark on a literary career. My father sent a letter to me at Bowdoin College, cautioning against such a course with the observation that there was not sufficient wealth in America to afford a living for a literary man. My father was a shrewd man. He began the letter with a practical warning, and ended it with a poetical criticism:

"I observe some poetry in the U.S. Literary Gazette," he wrote, "which, from the signature, I presume to be from your pen. It is a very pretty production, and I read it with pleasure. But you will observe that the second line of the sixth verse has too many feet." (5)

Q: Who did inspire you to become a writer?

A: My Grandfather, General Wadsworth whom I sometimes spent my summer holidays with on his farm wrote satirical verses. He was a capital storyteller and had a great fund of personal reminiscences of his Harvard and army days, his capture by the British and his escape from the Fort George at Castine. All these things had their effect upon my impressionable mind. (6)

Q: Have you always been passionate about walking?

A: Yes, it was always my chief exercise. When the snow was deep, I cut wood and found it rather irksome. As a makeshift for either, I once wrote to my father: "I have marked out an image upon my closet-door about my own size; and whenever I feel the want of exercise I strip off my coat, and, considering this image as in a posture of defence, make my motions as though in actual combat. This is a very classick amusement, and I have already become quite skilful as a pugilist." (7)

Q: Would you mind reading one of your poems?

A: I would be honoured:

THE BUILDERS

All are architects of Fate,
Working in these walls of Time;
Some with massive deeds and great,
Some with ornaments of rhyme.
Nothing useless is, or low;
Each thing in its place is best;
And what seems but idle show
Strengthens and supports the rest.
For the structure that we raise,
Time is with materials filled;
Our todays and yesterdays
Are the blocks with which we build
Truly shape and fashion these;
Leave no yawning gaps between;
Think not, because no man sees,
Such things will remain unseen.
In the elder days of Art,
Builders wrought with greatest care

Each minute and unseen part;
For the Gods see everywhere.
Let us do our work as well,
Both the unseen and the seen;
Make the house, where Gods may dwell,
Beautiful, entire and clean.
Else our lives are incomplete,
Standing in these walls of Time,
Broken stairways, where the feet
Stumble as they seek to climb.
Build today, then, strong and sure,
With a firm and ample base;
And ascending and secure
Shall tomorrow find its place.
Thus alone can we attain
To those turrets, where the eye
Sees the world as one vast plain,
And one boundless reach of sky. (8)

Q: You gathered an amazing collection of mementoes and showcased them in your home. Please tell me about them.

A: They were in my study where the quiet was only broken by the chimes of the old clock in the corner. A table in the centre of the room was heaped with books and paper in a look of orderly disorder, which I am certain any writer in your time can relate to.

Upon the same table, a treasure was Samuel Taylor Coleridge's inkstand with an early volume of his poems annotated in his own handwriting, which was as scraggly as that of a genius ought to be.

Among the pictures in the room, were crayon likenesses of Emerson, Sumner and Hawthorne, all taken when these famous men were in the flush of their youth.

We could spend all of this day discussing the things, which were displayed in my study. One cabinet alone contained a bit of Dante's coffin; a cylinder of some brilliant African beetles, two canes (one made from the spare of the ship on which "The Star Spangled Banner" was written and the other from "Acadie" and was surmounted by a hideous head which was my idea of "Evangeline." (9)

Q: Is it true another writer passed up the chance to write about "Evangeline"?

A: Yes, in fact a rector at a South Boston Church had been trying to induce Nathaniel Hawthorne to use the story. At a dinner with the two of them I said to Mr. Hawthorne, "If you really do not want this incident for a tale, then let me have it for a poem." I finished "Evangeline" in 1847. (10)

Q: There must also be a fascinating story regarding "The Ballad of the Schooner Hesperus"?

A: In December 17, 1839, I was plagued with toothache and dyspepsia. I recall writing to my father: "News of shipwrecks horrible on the coast. Twenty bodies washed ashore, near Gloucester, one lashed to a piece of the wreck. There is a reef called Norman's Woe where many of these took place; among others the schooner Hesperus...I must write a ballad about this."

Nearly a fortnight later I again took up my pen and wrote to my father, "I sat last evening till twelve o'clock by my fire, smoking, when suddenly it came into my mind to write the Ballad of the Schooner Hesperus, which I accordingly did. Then I went to bed but could not sleep. New thoughts were running in my mind, and I got up to add them to the ballad. It was three by the clock. I then went to bed and fell asleep. I feel pleased with the ballad. It hardly cost me any effort. It did not come into my mind by lines but by stanzas." (11)

Q: Might I join you in the recitation of your poem "The Arrow and The Song" as we make our way across the bridge?

A: Perfect choice my friend, perfect choice!

THE ARROW AND THE SONG

I shot an arrow into the air,

It fell to earth, I knew not where
For, so swiftly it flew, the sight
Could not follow it in its flight
I breathed a song into the air,
It fell to earth, I knew not where
For who has sight so keen and strong
That it can follow the flight of song?
Long, long afterward, in an oak
I found the arrow, still unbroken
And the song, from beginning to end,
I found again in the heart of a friend. (12)

Q: Do you have any advice for writers in the year 2003 and beyond?

A: In 1850 I wrote: If I wish to do anything in literature it must be done now. Few men have written good poetry after fifty. I believed it to be true and sound advice until in 1851, "The Golden Legend" was published. They printed 3500 copies, which sold out immediately. I was 56 years of age. It would seem as if thoughts, like children, have their periods of gestation, and then are born, whether we will or not. This was an observation I made after finishing "The Reaper and The Flowers." (13)

Q: Mr. Longfellow, I have enjoyed walking with you. However, I fear that both our time and this day are coming to an end. Would you mind reciting an appropriate poem for us? Perhaps one to close the curtains on this time we have shared?

A: Ah yes:

THE DAY IS DONE

The day is done, and the darkness
Falls from the wings of Night,
As a feather is wafted downward
From an eagle in his flight
I see the lights of the village

Gleam through the rain and the mist,
And a feeling of sadness comes o'er me
That my soul cannot resist
A feeling of sadness and longing,
That is not akin to pain,
And resembles sorrow only
As the mist resembles the rain
Come, read to me some poem,
Some simple and heartfelt lay,
That shall soothe this restless feeling,
And banish the thoughts of day
Not from the grand old masters,
Not from the bards sublime,
Whose distant footsteps echo
Through the corridors of Time
For like strains of martial music,
Their mighty thoughts suggest
Life's endless toil and endeavour
And tonight I long for rest
Read from some humbler poet,
Whose songs gushed from his heart,
As showers from the clouds of summer,
Or tears from the eyelids start
Who, through long days of labour,
And nights devoid of ease,
Still heard in his soul the music
Of wonderful melodies
Such songs have power to quiet
The restless pulse of care,
And come like the benediction
That follows after prayer.
Then read from the treasured volume
The poem of thy choice
And lend to the rhyme of the poet
The beauty of thy voice

And the night shall be filled with music,
And the cares that infest the day,
Shall fold their tents like the Arabs,
And as silently steal away. (14)

Mr. Longfellow stayed, lingering, drifting gently from my sight holding my hand in his. Our spirits parted, and no other tribute could be more befitting than the one the Honourable J. D. Long wrote upon Mr. Longfellow's death:

"It is a poor commonplace to say that Longfellow is the poet of the people, for no poet is a great or true poet, who is not that. Lives of great men all remind us not so much that we can make our lives sublime, as that our lives ARE sublime, if only we will not cumber or debase them.

Not by putting into melody something that is beyond and above you and me, not by breathing a music so exquisite that it never trembles in our fancies and prayers, does the poet rise to excellence; but by voicing the affections, the finer purpose, the nobleness, that are in the great common nature, - in the sailor up in the shrouds, in the maiden lashed to the floating mast, in the mother laying away her child, in the schoolboy at his task or play, or counting the sparks that fly from the blacksmith's forge, in the man at his work or when he rests from it, raided by blue-eyed banditti from the stairway and the hall.

So, the poet teaches us not our disparity from him, but our level with him, not our meanness, but our loftiness. The music he wrote is all lying unwritten in us. Let us sing it in our lives, which we can as he sung it from his pen, which we cannot." (15)

You'll want to read all of his works, but here's a list of some of my favourites which will get you started.

Evangeline
Hiawatha
The Wreck of the Hesperus
A Psalm of Life

Excelsior
Hymn to the Night
My Lost Youth
The Slave's Dream
The Light of Stars
Footsteps of Angels
The Spirit of Poetry
The Goblet of Life.

Good-bye for now!
Cathy McGough
Your Interviewer of Legendary Writers From Beyond

Chapter Sixteen

"THE BANJO" PATERSON RETURNS

To celebrate Australia Day 2002, (January 26) we have decided to contact A. B. "Banjo" Paterson. Mr. Paterson was born on February 17th, 1864 at Narambla, New South Wales.

While Madame Delatour was preparing to contact Mr. Paterson, I took the opportunity to read his most famous work – "Waltzing Matilda" which was written in 1895 in Queensland. For your reading convenience, I have included asterisks for words you may question the meaning of. You will find the definitions just below the ballad.

WALTZING MATILDA

Oh, there once was a *swagman camped in the *billabongs,
Under the shade of a *Coolabah tree
And he sang as he looked at the old *billy boiling,
"Who'll come a-waltzing Matilda with me?"
CHORUS
Who'll come a-waltzing Matilda, my darling?
Who'll come a-waltzing Matilda with me?

Waltzing Matilda and leading a water-bag,
Who'll come a-waltzing Matilda with me?
Up came the *jumbuck to drink at the waterhole,
Up jumped the swagman and grabbed him in glee
And he sang as he put him away in his *tucker-bag,
"You'll come a-waltzing Matilda with me."
Repeat CHORUS

Up came the *squatter a-riding his thoroughbred;
Up came policemen – one, two, and three.
"Whose is the jumbuck you've got in the tucker-bag?
You'll come a-waltzing Matilda with we."
Repeat CHORUS
Up sprang the swagman and jumped in the waterhole,
Drowning himself by the Coolabah tree;
And his voice can be heard as it sings in the billabongs,
"Who'll come a-waltzing Matilda with me?" (1)
Repeat CHORUS

*Swagman = Similar to a Hobo - A man who crossed the outback on foot doing odd-jobs in exchange for food or money. Why "Swagman?" Named for his "Swag Roll" – Similar to a backpack, which he strapped over his shoulders and in which he carried all his worldly possessions.

*Billabong = A waterhole.

*Coolabah = The native Eucalypt (Eucalyptus micro theca).

*Billy = A Kettle

*Jumbuck = A mal sheep (Aboriginal "jump up")

*Squatter = A person who illegally occupies another person's

property *Tuckerbag = Like a lunch bag.

Madame Delatour notified me, that Mr. Paterson would be arriving presently and without further ado there he was.

He had short, black hair, parted at the side and dark friendly eyes. He was wearing a navy-blue suit, white shirt with a high collar, a blue cravat, and a leather hat, which he tipped to greet me. (2)

He breathed in the smell of the gum trees surrounding our balcony and leaned forward watching the trail that winds along in front of our house. He obviously was hoping to see a horse or two galloping on by, tossing up the red Australian soil with its hooves. Instead, a young man who zipped by on a motorized scooter spellbound him! He sipped a glass of iced tea awaiting my first question.

Q: How did you come to be known as "The Banjo?"

A: I adopted the penname after a racehorse my family owned. When I was twenty-two years old, I wrote my first signed contribution and it was published in "The Bulletin" on June 12th, 1886. The ballad was "The Bush Fire" and after that the name just stuck. (3)

Q: J. F. Archibald founded "The Bulletin" in 1800 and there are stories about him being very harsh. How was your first meeting with him?

A: J. F. was always on the look-out for new writers and came across some of my works. I was called to his office and off I went and climbed a grimy flight of stairs at 24 Pitt St., until I stood before a door marked Mr. Archibald, Editor. On the door was pinned a spirited drawing of a gentleman lying quite loose on the strand with a dagger through him and on the drawing was written: "Archie, this is what will happen to you if you don't use my drawing about the policeman!" It cheered me up a lot. Evidently this was a free and easy place.

In an interview of ten minutes he said he would like me to try some more verse. Did I know anything about the bush? I told him that I had been reared there.

"All right," he said, "have a go at the bush. Have a go at anything that strikes you. Don't write anything like other people if you can help it. Let's see what you can do." (4)

Q: Bush Songs were popular at the time, but you turned them into Anthems.

A: Bush Songs should be heard to an accompaniment of clashing shears when the voice of a shearer rises through the din caused by the rush and bustle of a shearing shed, the scrambling of the sheep in their pens, and the hurry of the pickers-up; or when, on the roads, the cattle are restless on their camp at night and the man on watch, riding round them, strikes up "Bold Jack Donahue" to steady their nerves a little...The true bushman never hurries his songs. They are designed expressly to pass the time on long journeys or slow, wearisome rides after sheep or tired cattle; so, the songs are sung conscientiously through – chorus and all – and the last three words of the song are always spoken, never sung. (5)

Q: Would you do us the honour of reciting one of your ballads for us? What about a railroad song?

A: A request, how about that!

THE FLYING GANG

I served my time, in the days gone by,
In the railway's clash and clang,
And I worked my way to the end,
and I was the head of the 'Flying Gang'
Twas a chosen band that was kept at hand
in case of an urgent need,
was it south or north we were started forth
and away at our utmost speed.
If word reached town that a bridge was down,
The imperious summons rang –
"Come out with the pilot engine sharp,
and away with the flying gang."
Then a piercing scream and a rush of steam
As the engine moved ahead,
With a measured beat by the slum and street
Of the busy town we fled,
By the uplands bright and the homesteads white,
With the rush of the western gale,

And the pilot swayed with the pace we made
As she rocked on the ringing rail.
And the country children clapped their hands
As the engine's echoes rang,
But their elders said, "There is work ahead
When they send for the flying gang."
Then across the miles of the saltbush plain
That gleamed with the morning dew,
Where the grasses waved like the ripening grain
The pilot engine flew,
A fiery rush in the open bush
Where the grade marks seemed to fly,
And the order sped on the wires ahead,
The pilot must go by.
The Governor's special must stand aside,
And the fast express go hang,
Let your orders be that the line is free
For the boys of the flying gang. (6)

Q: I'm hoping to interview Rudyard Kipling sometime soon and I believe he was one of your mates. Have you any advice for me?

A: One expects a great literary genius, such as Kipling, to be in some way a sort of freak: drink, women, temperament, idleness, irregularity of habits – nearly all of the great writers of the past had one or other of these drawbacks, and some of them have had them all. Byron's life consisted mostly of purple patches; and Swinburne was not the hero of the song about the good young man that died. So, when I went to stay with Kipling in England, I was prepared for literally anything.

Kipling hated publicity and in private life he was just a hard-working, common sense, level-headed man, without any redeeming vices that I could discover. A pity too, perhaps; for there is nothing so interesting as scandals about great geniuses. (7)

Q: I believe Mr. Kipling visited Australia; did he tell you what he thought of it?

A: Yes, he said, "I must buy a house in Australia someday. I've a house in New York, and in Cape Town; but I'd like to live in Australia for a while. I've been there, but I only went through it like the devil went through Athlone, in standing jumps. You can't learn anything about a country that way. You have to live there and then you can get things right. You people in Australia haven't grown up yet. You think the "Melbourne Cup" is the most important thing in the world." (8)

Q: You also made the acquaintance of a young Winston Churchill?

A: A war correspondent, in army eyes, is an evil to be tolerated. Being an Australian, a steeplechase rider and polo player, I had a (possibly fictitious) reputation as a judge of a horse and was constantly asked to go and pick horses for officers of the remount depots. In that way, I got to know such celebrities as Lord Roberts, French, Haig, Churchill and Kipling, and I attained a status in the army that I would never have reached as a correspondent.

Churchill had such a strong personality that even in those early days, when he was quite a young man, the army were prepared to bet that he would either get into jail or become Prime Minister. He had done some soldiering; but he had an uncanny knack of antagonising his superior and inferior officers. (9)

Q: Mr. Paterson, many of your characters were so down-to-earth that your readers believed you were writing about people you knew. Was there really a man from Snowy River?"

A: "The Man from Snowy River" ... was written to describe the cleaning up of the wild horses in my own district. To make a job of it I had to create a character, to imagine a man who would ride better than anybody else, and where would he come from except from the Snowy? And what sort of horse would he ride except a half-thoroughbred mountain pony? I felt sure there must have been a man from Snowy River, and I was right. They have turned up from all the mountain districts – men who did exactly the same ride and could give you chapter and verse for every mile they descended and every creek they crossed. It was no small satisfaction that there really had been a man from Snowy River – more than one of them... (10)

Q: My son Simon loves many of the poems you have written for children. His favourites are the ones about the flying squirrels and the platypus. If I call him, would you mind reading to him?

A: It would be my pleasure.

I excused myself from the balcony and explained to my five-year old son Simon that he would be meeting "The Banjo" Paterson. Simon was dressed in his Spiderman costume and received what appeared to be a firm handshake from Mr. Paterson. "The Banjo" then invited Simon to sit upon his knee while he recited his poems:

FLYING SQUIRRELS

On the rugged water-shed
At the top of the bridle track
Where years ago, as the old men say,
The splitters went with a bullock-dray
But never a dray came back
At the time of the gum tree bloom,
When the scent in the air is strong,
And the blossom stirs in the evening breeze,
You may see the squirrels among the trees,
Playing the whole night long.
Never a care at all
Bothers their simple brains
You can see them glide in the moonlight dim

From tree to tree and from limb to limb,
Little grey aeroplanes
Each like a dormouse sleeps
In the spout of a gum tree old,
A ball of fur with a silver coat
Each with a tail around his throat
For fear of his catching a cold.
These are the things he eats,
Asking his friends to dine:
Moths and beetles and newborn shoots,
Honey and snacks of the native fruits,
And a glass of dew for wine (11)

Simon clapped his hands while "The Banjo" flipped through the book until he found the one he wanted to read:

OLD MAN PLATYPUS
Far from the trouble and toil of town,
Where the reed-beds sweep and shiver,
Look at the fragment of velvet brown –
Old Man Platypus drifting down,
Drifting along the river.
And he plays and dives in the river bends
In a style that is most elusive
With few relations and fewer friends,
For Old Man Platypus descends
From a family most elusive
He shares his burrow beneath the bank
With his wife and his son and daughter
At the roots of the reeds and the grasses rank;
And the bubbles show where our hero sank
To its entrance under water
Safe in the burrow below the falls
They live in a world of wonder,
Where no one visits and no one calls,
They sleep like little brown billiard balls

With their beaks tucked neatly under.

Mr. Paterson sensed it was time for him to go. Not wanting to frighten Simon – he gently patted him on the head and passed him over to me. He walked down the corridor and out of Simon's sight. Then he turned, smiled, tipped his hat – and vanished. I was pulled back to reality when Simon tugged at my shirt. He was growing impatient regarding ending his beloved poem:

And he talks in a deep unfriendly growl
As he goes on his journey lonely
For he's no relation to fish nor fowl,
Nor to bird nor beast, nor to horned owl;
In fact, he's the one and only! (12)

Simon and I continued reading on into the night, until he fell asleep in my arms. I don't think Simon realizes the significance of meeting "The Banjo" Paterson in his very own home. Perhaps one day he will.

Mate, read these... They are all bonzer!

The Man From Snowy River and Other Verses
Saltbush Bill J.P. and Other Verses
Singer of the Bush
Song of the Pen
Banjo Paterson – A Children's Treasury
Banjo Paterson's Australians
Snowy River Riders
Three Elephant Power and Other Stories
Old Schooldays
The Man Who Was Away
The Pannikin Poet
The Rhyme of the O'Sullivan
The Road to Gundagai
The Bushfire – An Allegory
A Dream of the Melbourne Cup
Clancy Overflow
The Hypnotist.

Hoo-roo!
Cathy McGough
Your Interviewer of Legendary Writers From Beyond

Chapter Seventeen

THOREAU ON WALKABOUT

Today, we will be sharing a morning walkabout with a man who had a poet's soul. His name is Henry David Thoreau, and he was born on July 12, 1817 in Concord, Massachusetts. When he died, at age 45, his two published books had sold miserably. For Henry David Thoreau, surely did walk "to the sound of a different drummer."

(Excuse me one moment, while I check on Madame Delatour's progress in contacting Mr. Thoreau.)

Apparently, Madame Delatour has been unable to reach Mr. Thoreau this morning, although he agreed to do an interview with us today. She suggested I begin walking, and she will bring him along to catch up with me presently.

Feeling a little stir-crazy, I agreed to this idea and was very glad to get out into the morning air. I'm not really a "morning person" – but once the air hits me, I can usually keep up with the best of them.

I began walking down the path, past the gum trees as I spied a baby kookaburra sitting in its arms. I stopped to make the sound of a kookaburra, but it did not recognize my distorted version of its laugh and paid me little attention. Lizards ran haphazardly as I moved along the driveway and out onto the street.

I stopped momentarily to ponder which route Mr. Thoreau would enjoy the most and decided to cross part of the way over the bridge and wait for him there.

I stood upon the bridge, looking down while the sun danced upon my rippling reflection. I recited one of Mr. Thoreau's poems aloud:

THE FISHER'S BOY
My life is like a stroll upon the beach,
As near the ocean's edge as I can go
My tardy steps its waves sometimes o'er-reach,
Sometimes I stay to let them overflow.
My sole employment is, and scrupulous care,
To place my gains beyond the reach of tides, -
Each smoother pebble, and each shell more rare,
Which Ocean kindly to my hand confides.
The middle sea
At this point Mr. Thoreau finished the final stanza
The middle sea contains no crimson dulse,
Its deeper waves cast up no pearls to view
Along the shore my hand is on its pulse,
And I converse with many a shipwrecked crew. (1)

Madame Delatour and I applauded vigorously. Mr. Thoreau removed his cap and bowed. I extended my hand, welcoming him to Cooks River, in Sydney, Australia but he didn't seem to notice me. Madame Delatour had his full attention.

Mr. Thoreau complimented Madame on her charming appearance. He lifted her hand and held it against his heart all the while looking deeply into her eyes. He took her hand, and kissed it passionately asking if her hand was "promised" to anyone.

Madame Delatour is rarely at a loss for words but this time she could not speak. She took care, not to offend Mr. Thoreau who was not her type, mumbled something, and bid us adieu. I've never seen anyone with 3" high heels walk so fast!

Mr. Thoreau watched Blanchetta disappear from his sight and then joined me in a stroll across the wooden bridge. A fish jumped, seeming to wave its tail in a greeting and Mr. Thoreau stopped to wave back at it.

It was nearly 6 a.m., and Mr. Thoreau paid me a compliment. He assumed since I was out and about during the wee hours of the morn this was my regular routine.

I hated to spoil his illusion – but felt the need to confess which I did, and this was his reply:

Morning air! If you will not drink of this at the fountainhead of the day, why, then we must even bottle up some and sell it in the shops, for the benefit of those who have lost their subscription ticket to morning time in this world!

You must learn to reawaken and keep yourself awake, not by mechanical aids, but by an infinite expectation of the dawn, which does not forsake you in your soundest sleep. I know of no more encouraging fact than the unquestionable ability of man to elevate his life by a conscious endeavour. It is something to be able to paint a particular picture, or to carve a statue, and so to make a few objects beautiful; but it is far more glorious to carve and paint the very atmosphere and medium through which we look, which morally we can do. To affect the quality of the day, that is the highest of arts. Every man is tasked to make his life, even in its details, worth of the contemplation of his most elevated and critical hour. If we refused, or rather used up, such paltry information as we get, the oracles would distinctly inform us how this might be done. (2)

I explained the theory of being a "morning person" as opposed to being an "afternoon" or "evening person" ... how some folks are not quite sociable until a certain time of the day. To this, he exclaimed:

Pshhha! Soon you will tell me, you feel comfortable walking along rugged trails - wearing totally inappropriate shoes for the task!

I looked down at my pair of black, ankle high boots with their cute little 2 in. spiked heel and could not help but laugh.

Q: Since we've already broached upon the subject, what is your opinion on fashion?

A: The head monkey at Paris puts on a traveller's cap and all the monkeys in America do the same. The principal object is, not that mankind may be well and honestly clad, but, unquestionably, that the corporations may be enriched. (3)

Q: Things have not changed much even today Mr. Thoreau. The world still clamours after the latest fashions, some of which would shock you! How do you feel about change?

A: All change is a miracle to contemplate; but it is a miracle, which is taking place every instant. Confucius said, "To know that we know what we know, and that we do not know what we do not know, that is true knowledge." When one man has reduced a fact of the imagination to be a fact to his understanding, I foresee that all men will at length establish their lives on that basis. (4)

Q: Would you mind reading a poem for us?

A: I dedicate this one to you Cathy:

FRIENDSHIP

I think awhile of Love, and while I think,
Love is to me a world,
Sole meat and sweetest drink,
And close connecting link
Tween Heaven and earth.
I only know it is, not how or why,
My greatest happiness;
However hard I try,

Not if I were to die,
Can I explain.
I fain would ask my friend how it can be,
But when the time arrives,
Then Love is more lovely
Than anything to me,
And so I'm dumb.
For if the truth were known, Love cannot speak,
But only thinks and does;
Though surely out 'twill leak
Without the help of Greek,
Or any tongue.
A man may love the truth and practise it,
Beauty he may admire,
And goodness not omit,
As much as may befit
To reverence.
But only when these three together meet,
As they always incline,
And make one soul the seat,
And favourite retreat,
Of loveliness;
When under kindred shape, like loves and hates
And a kindred nature,
Proclaim us to be mates,
Exposed to equal fates
Eternally;
And each may other help, and service do,
Drawing Love's bands more tight,
Service he ne'er shall rue
While one and one make two,
And two are one;
In such case only doth man fully prove
Fully as man can do,
What power there is in Love

His inmost soul to move
Resistlessly.
Two sturdy oaks I mean, which side by side,
Withstand the winter's storm,
And spite of wind and tide,
Grow up the meadow's pride,
For both are strong
Above they barely touch, but undermined
Down to their deepest source,
Admiring you shall find
Their roots are intertwined
Insep'rably. (5)

Q: I enjoyed reading your book "WALDEN" very much. I couldn't help but envy your unique situation and your courage. What was the most important thing you learned?

For those of you who do not know, Mr. Thoreau took himself off to Walden Pond where he built himself a cabin in which he lived off the land from 1845-47.

A: I learned; that if one advances confidently in the direction of his dreams, and endeavours to live the life which he has imagined, he will meet with a success unexpected in common hours. He will put some things behind, will pass an invisible boundary; new, universal, and more liberal laws will begin to establish themselves around and within him; or the old laws be expanded and interpreted in his favour in a more liberal sense, and he will live with the license of a higher order of beings. In proportion as he simplifies his life, the laws of the universe will appear less complex, and solitude will not be solitude, nor poverty, poverty, nor weakness, weakness. If you have built castles in the air, your work need not be lost; that is where they should be. Now put the foundations under them. (6)

Q: You built your own garret at "Walden," do you recommend taking on such a task to others?

A: There is some of the same fitness in a man's building his own house that there is in a bird's building its own nest. Who knows but if men constructed their dwellings with their own hands, and provided food for themselves and families simply and honestly enough, the poetic faculty would be universally developed, as birds universally sing when they are so engaged? But alas! We do like cowbirds and cuckoos, which lay their eggs in nests which other birds have built and cheer no traveller with their chattering and unmusical notes. (7)

Q: Some are builders; some are dreamers – surely you do not believe that every person has the capability to do what you did?

A: Every child begins the world again, to some extent, and loves to stay outdoors, even in the wet and cold. It plays house, as well as horse, having an instinct for it. Who does not remember the interest with which when young he looked at the shelving rocks or any approach to a cave? It was the natural yearning of that portion of our most primitive ancestor, which still survived from us. From the cave we have advanced to roofs of palm trees, of bark and boughs, of linen woven and stretched, of grass and straw, of boards and shingles, of stones and tiles. At last, we know not what it is to live in the open air, and our lives are domestic in more senses than we think. From the heart to the field is a great distance. It would be well perhaps if we were to spend more of our days and nights without any obstruction between us and the celestial bodies, if the poet did not speak so much from under a roof, or the saint dwell there so long. Birds do not sing in caves, nor do doves cherish their innocence in dovecots. (8)

Q: My son is beginning his education this year, and already my husband and I are fretting about his future. Have you any advice for us?

A: If I wished a boy to know something about the Arts and Sciences, for instance, I would not pursue the common course, which is merely to send him into the neighbourhood of some professor, where anything is professed and practised but the art of life; - to survey the world through a telescope or a microscope, and never with his natural eye; to study Chemistry, and not learn how his bread is made or Mechanics, and not learn how it is earned; to discover new satellites to Neptune, and not detect the motes in his eyes, or to what vagabond he is a satellite himself; or to be devoured by the monsters that swarm all around him, while contemplating the monsters in a drop of vinegar.

Which would have advanced the most at the end of the month, - the boy who had made his own jack knife from the ore which he had dug and smelted, reading as much as would be necessary for this, - or the boy who had attended the lectures on metallurgy at the Institute in the meanwhile, and had received a Rogers' penknife from his father? Which would be most likely to cut his fingers? (9)

Q: Thank you for your advice. There is no doubt which boy I would prefer my son to be. Mr. Thoreau, you spent a time in prison. Could describe what happened and why you were there?

A: I paid no poll tax for six years. I was put into a jail once on this account, for one night; and, as I stood considering the walls of solid stone, two or three feet thick, the door of wood and iron, a foot thick, and the iron grating which strained the light, I could not help but being struck with the foolishnesses of that institution which treated me as if I were mere flesh and blood and bones, to be locked up. I wondered that it should have concluded at length that this was the best use it could put me to and had never thought to avail itself of my services in some way.

I saw that, if there was a wall of stone between me and my townsmen, there was still a more difficult one to climb or break through before, they could get to be as free as I was. I did not for a moment feel confined, and the walls seemed a great waste of stone and mortar. I felt as if I alone of all my townsmen had paid my tax. They plainly did not know how to treat me but behaved like persons who are under bred. In every threat and in every compliment, there was a blunder; for they thought that my chief desire was to stand on the other side of that stonewall. I could not but smile to see how industriously they locked the door on my mediations, which followed them out again without let or hindrance, and they were really all that was dangerous. As they could not reach me, they had resolved to punish my body. I saw the State was half-witted and I lost all my remaining respect for it and pitied it. (10)

Q: If you never felt trapped, as they had intended you to feel, do you think you discovered some things about yourself, which otherwise you may never have known?

A: It was like travelling into a far country such as I had never expected to behold, to lie there for one night. It seemed to me that I never had heard the town-clock strike before, nor the evening sounds of the village; for we slept with the windows open, which were inside the grating. It was to see my native village in the light of the Middle Ages, and our Concord was turned into a Rhine stream, and visions of knights and castles passed before me. They were the voices of old burghers that I heard in the streets. I was an involuntary spectator and auditor of whatever was done and said in the kitchen of the adjacent village-inn – a wholly new and rare experience to me. It was a closer view of my native town. I was fairly inside of it. I never had seen its institutions before. This was one of its peculiar institutions; for it was a shire town. I began to comprehend what its inhabitants were about. (11)

Q: Were you elated to be released?

A: When I came out of prison – for someone interfered and paid the tax – I did not perceive that great changes had taken place on the common, such as he observed who went in a youth and emerged a tottering and grey-headed man; and yet a change had to my eyes come over the scene – the town, and State, and country – greater than any that mere time could effect. I saw yet more distinctly the State in which I lived. I saw to what extent the people among whom I lived could be trusted as good neighbours and friends; that their friendship was for summer weather only; that they did not greatly propose to do right; that they were a distinct race from me by their prejudices and superstitions. That they in their sacrifices to humanity ran no risks, not even to their property; that after all they were not so noble but they treated the thief as he had treated them, and hoped by a certain outward observance and a few prayers, and by walking in a particular straight though useless path from time to time, to save their souls. This may be to judge my neighbours harshly; for I believe that many of them were not aware that they had such an institution as a jail in their village. (12)

Q: Were you treated differently when you came back into society?

A: It was formerly the custom in our village, when a poor debtor came out of jail, for his acquaintances to salute him, looking through their fingers, which were crossed to represent the grating of a jail window, "How do ye do?"

My neighbours did not thus salute me, but first looked at me and then at one another, as if I had returned from a long journey. I was put into jail as I was going to the shoemakers to get a shoe, which was mended. When I was let out the next morning, I proceeded to finish my errand, and having put on my mended shoe, joined a huckleberry party, who were impatient to put themselves under my conduct; and in half an hour – for the horse was soon tackled – was in the midst of a huckleberry field, on one of our highest hills, two miles off, and then the State was nowhere to be seen. Such was the history of "My Prisons." (13)

Q: What in your estimation is the power of writing?

A: A written word is the choicest of relics. It is something at once more intimate with us and more universal than any other work of art. It is the work of art nearest to life itself. It may be translated into every language, and not only be read but actually breathed from all human lips; - not be represented on canvas or in marble only but be carved out of the breath of life itself. (14)

Q: Have you any advice to offer to readers of 2003 and beyond?

A: Simplicity, simplicity, simplicity! I say, let your affairs be as two or three, and not a hundred or a thousand; instead of a million count half a dozen, and keep your accounts on your thumbnail. Simplify, simplify. Instead of three meals a day, if it be necessary eat but one; instead of a hundred dishes, five; and reduce other things in proportion. However, mean your life is, meet it and live it; do not shun it and call it hard names. It is not so bad as you are. It looks poorest when you are richest. The faultfinder will find faults even in paradise. Love your life, poor as it is. You may perhaps have some pleasant, thrilling, glorious hours, even in a poorhouse. The setting sun is reflected from the windows of the alms-house as brightly as from the rich man's abode; the snow melts before its door as early in the spring. I do not see but a quiet mind may live as contentedly there, and have as cheering thoughts, as in a palace. (15)

Q: I don't know how much time is left, but I would like to hear you recite another poem or two?

A: These two-walk hand in hand:

SMOKE

LIGHT-WINGED Smoke, Icarian bird,
Melting thy pinions in thy upward flight;

Lark without song, and messenger of dawn,
Circling above the hamlets as thy nest;
Or else, departing dream, and shadowy form
Of midnight vision, gathering up thy skirts;
By night star-veiling, and by day
Darkening the light and blotting out the sun;
Go thou, my incense, upward from this hearth,
And ask the gods to pardon this clear flame.

MIST

LOW-ANCHORED cloud,
Newfoundland air,
Fountain-head and source of rivers,
Dew-cloth, dream-drapery,
And napkin spread by fays;
Drifting meadow of the air,
Where bloom the daisied banks and violets,
And in whose fenny labyrinth
The bittern booms and heron wades;
Spirit of lakes and seas and rivers,
Bear only perfumes and the scent
Of healing herbs to just men's fields. (16)

Q: Mr. Thoreau, thank you for enlightening my spirit with your words. You are a true Poet's Poet. You are beginning to fade, and indeed your time is running out.

A: Time is but the stream I go a-fishing in. I drink at it; but while I drink, I see the sandy bottom and detect how shallow it is. Its thin current slides away, but eternity remains. I would drink deeper; fish in the sky whose bottom is pebbly with stars. I cannot count one. (17)

Henry David Thoreau disappeared once more. I expect he is appreciated more in Heaven, than ever he was here on earth. As my thoughts continued in that vein, suddenly through the trees like a wind song, Henry David Thoreau whispered:

If man does not keep pace with his companions, perhaps it is because he hears a different drummer. Let him step to the music which he hears, however measured or far away. It is not important that he should mature as soon as an apple tree or an oak. Shall he turn his spring into summer?

If the condition of things which we were made for is not yet, what were any reality, which we can substitute? We will not be shipwrecked on a vain reality. Shall we with pains erect a heaven of blue glass over ourselves, though when it is done, we shall be sure to gaze still at the true ethereal heaven far above, as if the former were not? (18)

I suggest that you read "Walden" first - then delve into the rest!

Walden
On the Duty of Civil Disobedience Pt. 1 & 2
Inspiration
Walking
Life Without Principle
The Dispersion of Seeds
Maine Woods
I Knew a Man By Sight
Pray to What Earth?
Epitaph on the World
A Week on the Concord and Merrimack Rivers
A Yankee in Canada
Sympathy
Free Love
To a Stray Fowl
The Summer Rain
The Black Knight
Friendship.

So long!
Cathy McGough
Your Interviewer of Legendary Writers From Beyond

Chapter Eighteen

LORD BYRON MAKES AN ENTRANCE

It was in July of 2001, when Madame Delatour brought Lord Byron to see me. (Or should I say, he brought us to see him.) Lord Byron was the only writer who requested the interview be held at a specified location of his choice.

Our destination was Croft-on-Tees, in North Yorkshire. Mr. Byron asked us to meet him at the Rectory (which I discovered is now called the Old Rectory.) He said he would appear from behind a curtained Milbanke pew. (1)

Once we arrived at Gatwick Airport in London, we made use of the facilities, grabbed some snacks and beverages and then went on to "Alamo Auto Rentals."

Madame Delatour was all a-flap about driving on the other side of the road – so I took the wheel and we were on our way. It was a very smooth drive, as we grew closer and closer to Yorkshire, we couldn't help but notice the starkness of the landscape all around us.

We pulled up to the Old Rectory, at 11 a.m. and went inside immediately. Madame Delatour set to work in calling Lord

Byron to us. He had given her specific instructions not to enter the curtained area, as he wanted to make an "entrance."

George Gordon Byron was born on January 22nd in 1788. He lived a life filled with controversy and sometimes mayhem. He was born in England, but went abroad to live, to escape from scandal and rumour mongering.

Lord Byron died on the 19th of April in 1824, and at his request his body was brought back to England. He was denied burial at The Poet's Corner in Westminster Abbey, and instead was buried in his family vault at Hucknall Torkard, in Nottinghamshire. Several years after his death, a committee to raise a memorial to Byron was prepared and offered to Westminster Abbey. This was also refused. (2)

I will read one of Lord Byron's poems while we wait:

WHEN WE TWO PARTED

When we two parted
In silence and tears,
Half broken-hearted,
To sever for years,
Pale grew thy cheek and cold,
Colder thy kiss;
Truly that hour foretold
Sorrow to this.
The dew of the morning
Sank chill on my brow -
It felt like the warning
Of what I feel now.
Thy vows are all broken,
And light is thy fame:
I hear thy name spoken,
And share in its shame.
They name thee before me,
A knell to mine ear;
A shudder comes o'er me -

Why wert thou so dear?
They know not I knew thee,
Who knew thee too well: -
Long, long shall I rue thee
Too deeply to tell.
In secret we met -
In silence I grieve
That thy heart could forget,
Thy spirit deceive.
If I should meet thee
After long years,
How should I greet thee? –
With silence and tears. (3)

Madame Delatour and I were beside ourselves in tears, when Lord Byron, stepped out from behind the screen, sweeping back the crimson curtain like he was expecting the rush of a bull from the other side. He wore a royal blue velvet suit, with ruffles on the cuffs and on the collar of a white shirt. He was striking in appearance, and moved towards us, taking first Madame Delatour's hand into his and lightly kissing it, and then doing the same to mine. He walked around the rectory, taking it in, almost as if he was looking for someone or something.

Madame Delatour (somewhat reluctantly) slipped out the back door, leaving myself and Lord Byron sitting alone in the front pew. The hard wood creaked as I sat down, and Lord Byron flung himself onto the pew like it was a sofa in his own home, looking up at me with his head resting upon his cupped hands.

Q: Might I ask, why you chose to be interviewed here?

Q: Have you researched this meeting? Pray tell me why you think I asked you here my lady?

A: I can only surmise. Is it because you were married to Lady Ann Isabella here in 1815?

A: Ah yes. Regrettably. I never did see anyone much improved by matrimony. All my coupled contemporaries were bald and discontented. Wordsworth and Southey both lost their hair and good humour; and the last of the two had a good deal to lose. (4)

Q: I'd like to know about your childhood. Please tell me about it.

A: I was born, as the nurses use to say, with a silver spoon in my mouth, it has stuck in my throat and spoiled my palate, so that nothing put into it is swallowed with much relish – unless it be cayenne. (5) Next question.

Q: You were just 20 years old when your poems were first included in a collection called "Juvenilia" in 1808. How did it feel to see your work in print?

A: I can still remember what it said in "The Edinburgh Review":

"The Poesy of this young lord belongs to the class which neither gods nor men are said to permit. Indeed, we do not recollect to have seen a quantity of verse with so few deviations from that exact standard. His effusions are spread over a dead flat and can no more get above or below the level, than if they were so much stagnant water." (6)

I recollect the effect on me - it was rage and resistance, and redress – but not despondency nor despair. I grant that those are not amiable feelings; but, in this world of bustle and broil, and especially in the career of writing, a man should calculate upon his powers of resistance before he goes into the arena. (7)

Q: Is it true you never edited your work?

A: When I wrote, I wrote with rapidity and rarely with pains...When I first took pen in hand, I had to say what came uppermost or fling it away. I have always written as fast as I could put pen to paper, and never revised but in the proofs...I can never recast anything. I am like the tiger; if I miss the first spring, I go grumbling back to my jungle. (8)

Johnson showed us that no poetry is perfect; but to have corrected my work would have been a Herculean labour. In fact, I never looked beyond the moment of composition, and published merely at the request of my friends. (9)

Q: I recently discovered a rare copy of "Juvenilia" on-line the other day. Can you guess the price? It was 2500 pounds!

Q: What is on-line?

I reached into my briefcase and pulled out my laptop, powered it up and showed it to him. He watched in amazement as I typed in the words to one of his poems.

A: It is a communication device and writers like me record everything on here. You do not need pen or paper. It is all stored in the computer's memory bank.

A: It looks like devilry to me!

Lord Byron stood up and walked onto the altar. He waited behind the pulpit. I soon realized he wanted me to put the "devilry" away and give him my full attention.

ON THIS DAY I COMPLETE MY THIRTY-SIXTH YEAR

'Tis time the heart should be unmoved,
Since others it hath ceased to move:
Yet, though I cannot be beloved,
Still let me love!
My days are in the yellow leaf;
The flowers and fruits of love are gone;
The worm, the canker, and the grief
Are mine alone!
The fire that on my bosom preys
Is lone as some volcanic isle;
No torch is kindled at its blaze--
A funeral pile.
The hope, the fear, the jealous care,
The exalted portion of the pain
And power of love, I cannot share,

But wear the chain.
But 'tis not thus--and 'tis not here--
Such thoughts should shake my soul nor now,
Where glory decks the hero's bier,
Or binds his brow.
The sword, the banner, and the field,
Glory and Greece, around me see!
The Spartan, borne upon his shield,
Was not more free.
Awake! (not Greece--she is awake!)
Awake, my spirit! Think through whom
Thy life-blood tracks its parent lake,
And then strike home!
Tread those reviving passions down,
Unworthy manhood! — unto thee
Indifferent should the smile or frown
Of beauty be.
If thou regret'st thy youth, why live?
The land of honourable death
Is here: --up to the field, and give
Away thy breath!
Seek out--less often sought than found--
A soldier's grave, for thee the best;
Then look around, and choose thy ground,
And take thy rest. (10)

Q: You have a beautiful voice Lord Byron. Have you ever tried singing?

A: When I was at Aston, on my first visit, I had the habit, in passing my time a good deal alone, of -- I won't call it singing, for that I never attempt except to myself -- but of uttering, to what I think tunes, your "Oh breathe not," "When the last glimpse," and "When he who adores thee," with others of the same minstrel; -- they are my matins and vespers. I assuredly did not intend them to be overheard, but, one morning, in comes, not La Donna, but Il Marito, with a very grave face, saying, “Byron, I must request you won't sing any more, at least of those songs.” I stared, and said, “Certainly, but why?” – “To tell you the truth,” quoth he, “they make my wife cry, and so melancholy, that I wish her to hear no more of them.” (11)

Q: Is it true “Zuleika” almost didn’t make it to publication?

A: A friend once advised me (without seeing it, by the by) not to publish “Zuleika”; I believed he was right, but experience might have taught him that not to print is physically impossible. It is a horrible thing to do too frequently; --better print and they who like may read, and if they don't like, you have the satisfaction of knowing that they have, at least, purchased the right of saying so. (12)

Q: What is your opinion on William Shakespeare?

A: Shakespeare's name, you may depend on it, stands absurdly too high and will go down. He had no invention as to stories, none whatever. He took all his plots from old novels, and threw their stories into a dramatic shape, at as little expense of thought as you or I could turn his plays back again into prose tales. That he threw over whatever he did write some flashes of genius, nobody can deny but this was all.

Suppose any one to have the dramatic handling for the first time of such ready-made stories as Lear, Macbeth, etc., and he would be a sad fellow, indeed, if he did not make something very grand of them.

As for his historical plays, properly historical, I mean, they were mere re-dressings of former plays on the same subjects, and in twenty cases out of twenty-one, the finest, the very finest things, are taken all but verbatim out of the old affairs. You think, no doubt, that a horse, a horse, my kingdom for a horse! is Shakespeare's. Not a syllable of it.

You will find it all in the old nameless dramatist. Could not one take up Tom Jones and improve it, without being a greater genius than Fielding? I, for my part, think Shakespeare's plays might be improved, and the public seem, and have seemed to think so too, for not one of his is or ever has been acted as he wrote it; and what the pit applauded three hundred years past, is five times out of ten not Shakespeare's, but Cibber's. (13)

Q: Did you have a special technique for bringing your Muse to you?

A: A friend and I together, would drink from six till midnight, a bottle of champagne and six bottles of claret and then:

I write this reeling,
Having got drunk exceedingly today
So that I seem to stand upon the ceiling. (14)

Lord Byron laughed as he took one of the goblets from the altar and pretended, he was sipping hungrily.

Q: Your satire "Childe Harold" took the world by storm. Tom Moore, your biographer wrote, "The effect was electric." Were you elated when you received the news?

A: I awoke one morning and found myself famous! (15)

CHILDE HAROLD

Stanzas #75 & #76

Are not the mountains, waves and skies, a part
Of me and of my soul, as I of them?
Is not the love of these deep in my heart
With a pure passion? Should I not condemn
All objects, if compared with these? And stem
A tide of suffering, rather than forego
Such feelings for the hard and worldly phlegm
Of those whose eyes are only turned below,
Gazing upon the ground, with thoughts, which dare not glow?

But this is not my theme; and I return
To that which is immediate, and require
Those who find contemplation in the urn,

To look on One, whose dust was once all fire,
A native of the land where I respire
The clear air for a while – a passing guest,
Where he became a being, - whose desire
Was to be glorious; 'twas a foolish quest,
The which to gain and keep, he sacrificed the rest. (16)

When he finished, I reached into my bag and took a quick swig of my bottle of Evian. I offered him a drink, and he examined the plastic bottle with some curiosity. I explained about the world's love for purchasing bottled water. As he pushed it back towards me, he murmured something about man's stupidity in the future...

Q: Is there any truth to the tale that you believed John Keats died because of a bad review in "The Quarterly"?

A: Shelley wrote an elegy on Keats, accusing "The Quarterly" of killing him:

Who killed John Keats?
I, says the Quarterly,
So savage and Tartarly;
'Twas one of my feats.
Who shot the arrow?
The poet-priest Milman
(So ready to kill man),
Or Southey or Barrow.

You know very well that I did not approve of Keats' poetry, or principles of poetry. His "Hyperion" is a fine monument and will keep his name. I do not envy the man who wrote the article: "The Quarterly's" review people have no more right to kill than any other foot pads. However, he who would die of an article in a review would probably have died of something else equally trivial. (17)

Q: Could you tell me about your friendship with Percy Bysshe Shelley?

A: He was the most companionable person under thirty that I ever knew. (18) He was, to my knowledge, the least selfish and the mildest of men - a man who had made more sacrifices of his fortune and feelings for others than any I ever heard of. (19)

Q: There are two legends still believed today about Mr. Shelley. One was about his heart, the other about what he had in his pocket when he drowned. Could you confirm or deny?

A: We burned the bodies of Shelley and Williams on the seashore, to render them fit for removal and regular interment. You could have no idea what an extraordinary effect such a funeral pile had, on a desolate shore, with mountains in the background and the sea before, and the singular appearance the salt and frankincense gave to the flame. All of Shelley was consumed, except his heart, which would not take the flame, and which we preserved in spirits of wine. On the other matter, it was not a Bible that was found in Shelley's pocket, but John Keats' poems. (20)

Q: Thank you. I appreciate your frankness. Did you choose to write, or did writing choose you?

A: Who would write, if he had anything better to do? I think the mighty stir made about scribbling and scribes, by themselves and others, a sign of effeminacy, degeneracy and weakness. (21)

I wrote "Bridge of Abydos" in four days. I wrote "Corsair" in ten days. I wrote "Lara" whilst undressing after balls and masquerades. I by no means rank poetry or poets high in the scale of imagination. Poetry is the lava of the imagination; whose eruption prevents an earthquake. If I had lived ten years longer, you would have seen that all was not over with me, - I don't mean in literature, for that is nothing, and, it may seem odd enough to say, I don't think it was my vocation. But you would have seen that I did something or other! Alas I was a poet by avocation and a pirate by vocation! (22)

But an' it were to do again, — I should write again, I suppose. Such is human nature, at least my share of it—though I shall think better of myself, if I would have had sense to stop now. (23)

Q: Do you recall a place in the churchyard, on Harrow Hill where there is a tombstone said to have been your favourite seat when meditating and composing?

He nodded in recognition of the place.

It needed to be guarded by an iron cage from your fervent admirers, who were destroying it and carrying away pieces in remembrance of you.

A: A part of the time passed there – was the happiest of my life. (24)

Q: Have you any advice for writers in the future?

A: Always laugh when you can. It is cheap medicine. I also offer words to live by from "Don Juan":

For words are things; and a small drop of ink
Falling like dew, upon a thought produces
That which makes thousands, perhaps millions, think. (25)

Q: Do you believe that absence makes the heart grow fonder?

A: I pondered the miseries of separation, that—oh how seldom we see those we love! Yet we live ages in moments, when met. The only thing that consoled me during absence was the reflection that no mental or personal estrangement, from ennui or disagreement, could take place; and when people met hereafter, even though many changes may have taken place in the meantime, still, unless they were tired of each other, they were ready to reunite, and did not blame each other for the circumstances that severed them. (26)

Q: You kept a journal for many years. Is it something you would recommend to other writers?

A: I was obliged to write a Journal, that which preserved me from verse, --at least from keeping it. I often threw poems into the fire (which was relighted to my great comfort), and then I smoked out of my head the plan of another. (27)

Q: Is life too short?

A: When one subtracts from life infancy (which is vegetation), --sleep, eating, and swilling—buttoning and unbuttoning—how much remains of downright existence? The summer of a dormouse. (28)

Q: What was your least favourite form to write in?

A: I once wrote two Sonnets. I never wrote but one sonnet before, and that was not in earnest, and many years ago, as an exercise—and I decided then that I would never write another. They were the most puling, petrifying, stupidly platonic compositions. I detested the Petrarch so much, that I would not be the man even to have obtained his "Laura", which the metaphysical, whining dotard never could. (29)

Madame Delatour popped her head around the corner, pointing anxiously to her watch and asking us to come outside. I had hoped Lord Byron would read another poem but was curious as to what or who was waiting for us outdoors.

In the end, curiosity gave in, and we ventured outside the Rectory. Waiting for Lord Byron was a large black steed, whose mane blew like a scarf in the wind. Lord Byron greeted the horse and jumped upon her back. He thanked us, for reuniting him with his "true love" and patted her sides fervently.

Q: Please don't go yet. There is still time enough for you to recite: "She Walks In Beauty."

A: Ladies, I will indeed recite the poem you have chosen, but in honour of this handsome friend of mine.

Lord Byron hugged his true love's raven mane. She replied with a "neigh" as he whispered:

SHE WALKS IN BEAUTY

She walks in beauty, like the night
Of cloudless climes and starry skies;

And all that's best of dark and bright
Meet in her aspect and her eyes:
Thus mellowed to that tender light
Which heaven to gaudy day denies.
One shade the more, one ray the less,
Had half impaired the nameless grace
Which waves in every raven tress,
Or softly lightens o'er her face;
Where thoughts serenely sweet express
How pure, how dear their dwelling-place.
And on that cheek, and o'er that brow,
So soft, so calm, yet eloquent,
The smiles that win, the tints that glow,
But tell of days in goodness spent,
A mind at peace with all below,
A heart whose love is innocent! (30)

When he said the last line, he kicked the sides of his horse and off they went into the noon hour sunshine. We could hear the hooves, clip clopping and Lord Byron singing something, as they vanished forever from the earth.

To find out more about Lord Byron's works I advise you seek out the following:

Childe Harold Pilgrimage
Don Juan
Prometheus
I Would I Were A Careless Child
All for Love
Oh! Snatched Away in Beauty's Bloom
Fare Thee Well
On This Day I Complete My Thirty Sixth Year!
Churchill's Grave
Lines on Hearing That Lady Byron Was Ill
Beauty's Bloom
So, We'll Go No More A'Roving
My Soul is Dark

Darkness
Stanzas for Music
The Prisoner of Chillon
A Spirit Passed Before Me
Solitude
There's Not a Joy The World Can Give
The Destruction of Sennacherib
Lines Inscribed Upon a Cup Formed from a Skull
To Thomas Moore
Lines Written Beneath an Elm in the Churchyard of Harrow.

I do hope Lord Byron's interview was well worth the wait.
Wes gesund!
Cathy McGough
Your Interviewer of Legendary Writers From Beyond

Chapter Nineteen

THE BEGINNING WITH BAUDELAIRE

When Madame Delatour and I first met, the unexpected appearance of Charles Baudelaire was quite a shock. Being a sceptic at heart, I examined the area for every kind of trickery imaginable. I walked around Monsieur Baudelaire and even shook his hand to be sure that he was real since he appeared out of thin air. I wondered if he was an actor, playing the part, but soon came to realize this was not so. For yes, he was the one and only Charles Baudelaire, born in Paris, France, on April 9, 1821.

After our meeting, Madame Delatour explained in more detail about her "gift" to me. Fortunately for us, Madame Delatour had begun carrying a small tape recorder with her in her purse to make a record of all encounters she made. Unbeknownst to me, when Monsieur Baudelaire made his appearance, she reached into her handbag and activated the tape recorder.

My dear reader, you may suggest we have made this recording illegally by infringing on Mr. Baudelaire's rights since he did not give us permission to record his voice.

Madame Delatour believed wasting crucial, but limited time explaining what a tape recorder was to Mr. Baudelaire - would have been impossible.

At the time of the recording, I was unaware of the recording device but fully support Madame Delatour's decision. Besides, you must remember that Monsieur Baudelaire is dead. (May he rest in peace.)

For the purpose of this re-enactment, I will be using Madame Delatour's tapes today. Madame Delatour was familiar with Mr. Baudelaire's works since he is indisputably one of France's most influential poets of all time. I too was familiar with some but not all his works – the most famous of which is "Les Fleurs du Mal" (Flowers of Evil) which was published in 1857. All involved – author, publisher and printer – were prosecuted and found guilty of obscenity and blasphemy. Six poems were deleted from the book. (1)

However, today "Les Fleurs du Mal" is one of the most frequently edited books in world of literature. It has been translated into many languages and is read throughout the world.

While we wait, how better to pass time than by reading:

BEAUTY

I am as beautiful, O mortals! As a dream of stone,
And my breast, on which each man is wounded in turn,
Is made to inspire in the poet a love
As eternal and mute as matter.
I preside in the heavens like a misunderstood sphinx;
I unite a heart of snow with the whiteness of swans;
I hate all movement, which displaces lines,
And I never weep and I never laugh.
The poets before my great poses,
Which I seem to borrow from the proudest monuments,
Will consume their days in austere studies;
For I have, in order to fascinate these docile lovers,

Pure mirrors which make all things more beautiful;
My eyes, my large eyes with their eternal light! (2)

Monsieur Charles Baudelaire arrived attired in black. He could easily have been mistaken for a mortician (or a corpse). His eyes revealed the heart of a man, who had lived a difficult and often lonely life. Monsieur Baudelaire seemed to know straightaway that it was Madame Delatour who had summoned him to meet with us at The Eiffel Tower and he walked towards us with a sense of familiarity.

Q: What are your thoughts on criticism?

A: I sincerely believe that the best criticism is that kind which is amusing and poetic; not the cold mathematical kind, which, on the pretext of explaining everything, shows neither hate nor love, and voluntarily rids itself of every trace of feeling; but rather – since a beautiful picture is nature as seen by an artist – that criticism which is the picture as seen by an intelligent sensitive spirit. Therefore, the best article on painting could be a sonnet or an elegy. But this kind of criticism is destined for poetry anthologies and readers of poetry.

Monsieur Baudelaire hesitated, looking at us briefly and then continued with:

My compliments to you two jeune filles regarding your make-up. Red and black symbolize life. The black lines give depth and strangeness to your expressions, and to your eyes they give a more specific appearance of a window opening unto the infinite; rouge, which colours your high cheek bones, increases even more the light of your eyeballs and adds to the beautiful face of a woman the mysterious passion of the priestess. (3)

Q: Madame Delatour and I blushed and giggled like young schoolgirls as we asked Monsieur Baudelaire about the importance of laughter.

A: The laughter of children is like the blossoming of a flower. It is the joy of receiving, the joy of breathing, the joy of opening out, the joy of contemplation, of living, of growing. It is the joy of a plant. Generally speaking, it is more like a smile, something analogous to the waving of the tail of dogs or the purring of cats. And yet, notice carefully that if the laughter of children still differs from the expressions of animal contentment, it is because that laughter is not completely devoid of ambition. (4)

Q: Monsieur Baudelaire, would you mind reading one of your stories for us?

A: I offer to you a story with a moral. The story of:

THE POOR BOY'S TOY

I want to convey the idea of an innocent diversion. There are so few pastimes, which are not blameworthy. When you leave the house in the morning, with the firm intention of strolling along the main streets, fill your pockets with those inexpensive small inventions, such as the flat jumping jack manipulated by a single string, blacksmiths striking the anvil, the rider with a horse whose tail is a whistle, - and offer them to the neglected and poor children you meet in front of restaurants where they stand by a tree. You will see their eyes grow immoderately big. At first, they won't dare take anything. They won't believe in their good luck. Then their hands will grab the present avidly, and they will run off like cats who go far away from you to eat the piece of food you gave them. These children have learned to distrust man.

On a road, behind the iron gate of a large garden at the end of which you could see the whiteness of an attractive castle lit up by the sun, there was a beautiful fresh-complexioned child, dressed in those country clothes which have so much fastidiousness.

Luxury, freedom from care, and the habitual display of wealth make those children so charming that you could believe them made from a different substance than the children of an undistinguished or poor class.

Beside him on the grass lay a magnificent toy, as beautiful as its master, varnished, gilded, clothed in a purple robe, and covered with plumes and beads. But the child was paying no attention to his favourite toy. This is what he was looking at.

On the other side of the iron gate, on the road, in the midst of thistles and nettles, there was another child, dirty, frail, sooty, one of those child-waifs whose beauty an impartial eye might discover if, as the eye of a connoisseur guesses the ideal of painting under a body varnish, it cleaned the child of the repulsive patina of poverty.

Through the symbolic bars separating two worlds, the main road and the castle, the poor child was showing his own toy to the rich child who was greedily examining it as if it were a rare and strange object. Now, this toy, which the small ragamuffin was irritating by shaking a wire box back and forth, was a live rat! His parents, for economy's sake doubtless, had gotten the toy from life itself.As the two children laughed fraternally at one another, they showed teeth of similar whiteness. (5)

Madame Delatour and I were gasping for breath because the tears were flowing down our cheeks. Monsieur Baudelaire was moved by our emotional outpour and began reciting a poem:

THE ALBATROSS

Often, as an amusement, crewmen
Catch albatrosses, huge birds of the sea,
Who follow, indolent companions of the voyage,
The ship gliding over the salty deeps.
As soon as they have placed them on the deck,
These kings of the sky, awkward and ashamed,
Pitiably let their large white wings
Drag at their sides like oars.
This winged voyager, how gauche and weak he is!
Once so handsome, how comic and ugly he is!
One sailor irritates his beak with a pipestem,

And mimes, as he limps, the invalid who once flew!
The Poet is like the prince of the clouds,
Who haunts the tempest and mocks the archer;
Exiled on the earth in the midst of derision,
His giant wings keep him from walking. (6)

Madame Delatour was able to pull herself together, but all I could picture was that lonely albatross with my head upon its body.

Q: Did you love drama and in specific, the Theatre?

A: In childhood and still today, the most beautiful thing I found in a theatre is the chandelier – a beautiful luminous crystalline, complicated, circular and symmetrical object. After all, the chandelier has always seemed to me the principal actor, either seen through the large end or the small end of opera glasses. (7)

Q: You adored the works of Edgar Allan Poe. Can you explain what it was about his writing, which intrigued you?

A: With Poe, the introductory part of each piece is attractive without violence, like a whirlwind. His solemnity surprises and keeps the reader's mind alert. At the very start you feel it is a question of something serious. And slowly, gradually, a story unfolds whose interest depends upon an imperceptible deviation of the intellect, on a bold hypothesis, on an imprudent dosage of Nature in the amalgam of the faculties. The reader, held by dizziness, is forced to follow the writer in his fascinating deduction. (8)

Regrettably the tape ends here. I recall Monsieur Baudelaire grasping his stomach and lurching forward momentarily and then becoming translucent.

Returning from whence he came seemed to be a painful process, one he was clearly resisting. Monsieur Baudelaire had unfinished business to attend to.

He moved towards the edge of the Eiffel Tower until the wind lifted his feet off the ground. He was carried thus, over the lip of the tower and out into the clouds. He pirouetted, gazing about him as he blew Paris a series of passionate kisses. And then he disappeared.

When I look back upon that moment now, I swear I saw the kisses taking form, floating from atop the Tower, on lower and lower, until the breeze picked them up and carried them onwards, down the River Seine, out among the crowds, to who knows where.

On the way down, Madame Delatour and I took the elevator. This was the first of many meetings with Legendary Writers from Beyond.

You must read Charles Baudelaire's works. You will not regret it! I stand by the following:

Salon 1845/1946
Black Venus
The Flowers of Evil
Carrion
To The Reader
Cats
Overcast
White Venus
Green Eyed Venus
Artificial Paradises
Paris Spleen
Elevation
Consecration
Guiding Lights
Even When She Walks
Wine of the Lovers.

Au Revoir Mon Ami!
Cathy McGough
Your Interviewer of Legendary Writers From Beyond

Chapter Twenty

THE CONCLUSION - NOT

Regrettably, I must inform you that our "Interviews With Legendary Writers From Beyond" have now concluded.

To those of you who have been strong supporters of this book from its inception and who previously read excerpts of it when it was in the form of a column I would like to speak directly.

Many of you have written, called, emailed and faxed us asking why no women writers were included in this book.

Before I go any further – let me assure you dear readers that I tried.

Due to Madame Delatour's rather flirtatious nature, (not to mention her status in being single) she had a very strong inclination for contacting Legendary Men Writers From Beyond.

Since she was in the driver's seat (so to speak) I agreed, somewhat reluctantly – hoping to one day change her mind. Unfortunately, no matter what I said or did – Madame would not budge an inch.

Presently, Madame Delatour is on strike and is in the process of looking for a formal body to negotiate her terms, i.e., Medium/Psychic's Union. So far there is no such thing, but I have a feeling she may start one up, if I do not agree to her terms.

What are her terms you ask? Cash, pure and simple. Madame Delatour sees Mediums out there – ones who do not possess anywhere near the powers, which she possesses. Yet they are earning millions of dollars every day on television. Madame Delatour would like a cut of that pie.

Let me remind you, as an interviewer, I receive no compensation. I do it purely for the love of the writers whom we are able to contact and interview. Suffice it to say, Madame Delatour and I will work something out and when we do, perhaps we'll do another interview (or two!)

Thank you for sharing in our interviews!

TTFN!
Cathy McGough (WRITTEN IN 2004)
Your Interviewer of Legendary Writers From Beyond

Chapter Twenty-One

A NEW INTERVIEW WITH VOLTAIRE IN 2006

This morning I awoke, to discover Interviews With Legendary Writers From Beyond was not a done deal. Suffice it to say Madame Delatour and I have worked something out having read the following poem which was written by François-Marie Arouet de Voltaire after a devastating earthquake hit Lisbon on All Saints' Day in 1755, which wiped out the lives of 30,000 people in just six minutes.

Madame Delatour, after explaining the recent Tsunami Disaster has agreed to an interview.

While we wait for his arrival, let me tell you about François-Marie Arouet de Voltaire who was born on November 21, 1694, in Paris, France. Monsieur Voltaire was a satirist who fought against the establishment using his pen as his weapon. His most famous work was written in 1759, "Candide," and is still performed today live in theatres all over the world.

Voltaire lived to be 84 years of age (died in Paris on May 30, 1778) and he was the leader of the Age of Enlightenment. He never stopped writing, right up to the end and left behind over 14,000 letters and over two thousand books and pamphlets. (1)

Madame Delatour informed me that Monsieur Voltaire was on his way. I awaited his arrival with great expectations.

Moments later when he walked towards me, I was struck instantly by his small stature. He was wearing a red coat lined with white ermine, white stockings and black boots with silver buckles. His most outstanding feature was his smile with which he greeted me. He then embraced me, like we were old friends and promptly began his recitation:

ON THE DISASTER OF LISBON

(Or an Examination of the Axiom, "All is Well")
Unhappy mortals! Dark and mourning earth!
Affrighted gathering of humankind!
Eternal lingering of useless pain!
Come, ye philosophers, who cry, "All's well,"
And contemplate this ruin of a world.
Behold these shreds and cinders of your race,
This child and mother heaped in common wreck,
These scattered limbs beneath the marble shafts—
A hundred thousand whom the earth devours,
Who, torn and bloody, palpitating yet,
Entombed beneath their hospitable roofs,
In racking torment end their stricken lives.
To those expiring murmurs of distress,
To that appalling spectacle of woe,
Will ye reply: "You do but illustrate
The iron laws that chain the will of God"?
Say ye, o'er that yet quivering mass of flesh:
"God is avenged: the wage of sin is death"?
What crime, what sin, had those young hearts conceived

That lie, bleeding and torn, on mother's breast?
Did fallen Lisbon deeper drink of vice
Than London, Paris, or sunlit Madrid?
In these men dance; at Lisbon yawns the abyss.
Tranquil spectators of your brothers' wreck,
Unmoved by this repellent dance of death,
Who calmly seek the reason of such storms,
Let them but lash your own security;
Your tears will mingle freely with the flood.
When earth its horrid jaws half open shows,
My plaint is innocent; my cries are just.
Surrounded by such cruelties of fate,
By rage of evil and by snares of death,
Fronting the fierceness of the elements,
Sharing our ills, indulge me my lament.
"T'is pride," ye say— "the pride of rebel heart,
To think we might fare better than we do."
Go, tell it to the Tagus' stricken banks;
Search in the ruins of that bloody shock;
Ask of the dying in that house of grief,
Whether t'is pride that calls on heaven for help
And pity for the sufferings of men.
"All's well," ye say, "and all is necessary."
Think ye this universe had been the worse
Without this hellish gulf in Portugal?
Are ye so sure the great eternal cause,
That knows all things, and for itself creates,
Could not have placed us in this dreary clime
Without volcanoes seething 'neath our feet?
Set you this limit to the power supreme?
Would you forbid it use its clemency?

He took a moment to catch his breath and then had a sip of water before he continued:

At fitful moments in our pain-racked life
The hand of pleasure wipes away our tears;

But pleasure passes like a fleeting shade,
And leaves a legacy of pain and loss.
The past for us is but a fond regret,
The present grim, unless the future's clear.
If thought must end in darkness of the tomb,
All will be well one day—so runs our hope.
All now is well, is but an idle dream.
The wise deceive me: God alone is right.
With lowly sighing, subject in my pain,
I do not fling myself 'gainst Providence.
Once did I sing, in less lugubrious tone,
The sunny ways of pleasure's genial rule;
The times have changed, and, taught by growing age,
And sharing of the frailty of mankind,
Seeking a light amid the deepening gloom
I can but suffer and will not repine.
A caliph once, when his last hour had come,
This prayer addressed to him he reverenced:
"To thee, sole and all-powerful king, I bear
What thou dost lack in thy immensity—
Evil and ignorance, distress and sin."
He might have added one thing further—hope. (2)

Voltaire and I wept together for those who were lost and kept a moment of silence and then our interview began.

Q: Did you enjoy school?

A: There I learned Latin and nonsense. I was not like other boys in that I did not join in. The Fathers at the Jesuits at the Collège Louis-le-Grand made many attempts to persuade me. I would say: everyone must jump after his own fashion. They soon left me alone. (3)

Q: Is that when you started writing?

A: I wrote some verses then, verses, which showed promise and originality of thought enough to attract the attention of my teacher. One in particular who disliked me immensely said, "Witch, you will one day be the standard bearer of Deism in France." This assessment did not help with my lack of popularity in the schoolyard. (4)

Q: You studied law from 1711-13 and then worked as a secretary to the Ambassador of Holland before you decided to dedicate your life to writing?

A: Ah, a decision I never once regretted. Alas, I was arrested in 1717, unjustly I might add and sent to the Bastille. It is bad enough being arrested and imprisoned – but for a crime I hadn't committed! I made use of the time by writing my first play: "Oedipe." I changed my name to Voltaire.

When eleven months later I was released from prison, this my first play, received rave reviews when it was staged which proves how work can save us from three great evils: boredom, vice and need. (5)

Q: Tell me what it was like writing with Censorship sitting like a vulture on your shoulder?

A: In 1723 an edict stated: "No publishers or others may print or reprint, anywhere in the kingdom, any books without having obtained permission in advance by letters sealed with the Great Seal." Official censors were required to testify that the book contained nothing contrary to religion, public order or sound morality. Books deemed to be illegal were burned; writer and printer were sent to prison.

Then in 1757, an assassination attempt was made on Louis XV. Chaos ensued and with it a new edict: "death was decreed for all those who shall be convicted of having written or printed any works intended to attack religion, to assail the royal authority, or to disturb the order and tranquillity of the realm." By 1764, books, pamphlets and even Prefaces, were scrutinized. (6)

Q: How did you live, knowing you could be caught at any moment?

A: I lived to escape. Not a moment went by when I wasn't thinking about how I would get away, what I would do if I heard they were seeking me out. I wrote anonymously most of the time.

Q: Yet, they knew it was you?

A: Knowing is one thing, proving is another! The sale of my work was forbidden; still my work was in demand. I and other writers sent out work to be printed in Amsterdam, The Hague, and Geneva. It was then smuggled into France and sought after. Hence this letter I wrote to the officials in June of 1733:

As you have it in your power, sir, to do some service to letters, I implore you not to clip the wings of our writers so closely, nor to turn into barn-door fowls those who, allowed a start, might become eagles; reasonable liberty permits the mind to soar! (7)

Q: When did you write your Philosophical Letters?

A: Having been exiled, I managed to stay out of trouble for three years and wrote essays about Epic Poetry and The Civil Wars in France, which were published in 1727. I returned to France and wrote plays, poetry, scientific treatises and became a royal historiographer.

My "Philosophical Letters" – in which I compared the French system of government with the English system, put me in hot water once more. My book was banned in France and I had to flee. It became a Best Seller in England. (8)

Q: You weren't impressed with Shakespeare?

A: Shakespeare boasted a strong fruitful genius. He was natural and sublime but had not so much as a single spark of good taste or knew one rule of the drama. I will now hazard a random, but, at the same time, true reflection, which is, that the great merit of this dramatic poet has been the ruin of the English stage. There are such beautiful, such noble, such dreadful scenes in this writer's monstrous farces, to which the name of tragedy is given, that they have always been exhibited with great success.

Time, which alone gives reputation to writers, at last makes their very faults venerable. Most of the whimsical gigantic images of this poet, have, through length of time acquired a right of passing for sublime. Most of the modern dramatic writers have copied him: but the touches and descriptions which are applauded in Shakespeare are hissed at in these writers; and you will easily believe that the veneration in which this author is held increases in proportion to the contempt which is shown to the moderns. Dramatic writers don't consider that they should not imitate him; and the ill-success of Shakespeare's imitators produces no other effect than to make him be considered inimitable.

The shining monsters of Shakespeare have infinite more delight than the judicious images of the moderns. Hitherto the poetical genius of the English resembles a tufted tree planted by the hand of Nature, that throws out a thousand branches at random, and spreads equally, but with great vigour. It dies if you attempt to force its nature, and to lop and dress it in the same manner as the trees of the Garden of Marli. (9)

Q: A problem in the translation perhaps?

A: We don't laugh when reading a translation. If you have a mind to understand the English comedy, the only way to do this will be for you to go to England, spend three years in London, to make yourself master of the English tongue, and to frequent the playhouse every night. I receive but little pleasure from the perusal of Aristophanes and Plautus, and for this reason because I am neither a Greek nor a Roman. The delicacy of humour, the allusion, the apropos – all these are lost to a foreigner.

Nothing is easier than to exhibit in prose all the silly impertinences, which a poet may have thrown out; but that it is a very difficult task to translate his fine verses. (10)

Q: What part does imagination play in writing poetry?

A: In poetry particularly imagination of detail and expression ought to prevail. It is always agreeable, but there it is necessary.

In Homer, Virgil, and Horace, almost all is imagery, without even the reader's perceiving it. Tragedy requires fewer images, fewer picturesque expressions and sublime metaphors and allegories than the epic poem and the ode; but the greater part of these beauties, under discreet and able management, produce an admirable effect in tragedy; they should never, however, be forced, stilted, or gigantic.

Active imagination, which constitutes poets, confers on them enthusiasm, according to the true meaning of the Greek word, that internal emotion which in reality agitates the mind and transforms the author into the personage whom he introduces as the speaker; for such is the true enthusiasm, which consists in emotion and imagery. An author under this influence says precisely what would be said by the character he is exhibiting.

Less imagination is admissible in eloquence than in poetry. The reason is obvious—ordinary discourse should be less remote from common ideas. The orator speaks the language of all; the foundation of the poet's performance is fiction. Accordingly, imagination is the essence of his art; to the orator it is only an accessory. (11)

Q: Monsieur Voltaire, our time is quickly coming to an end. Have you thought of any further advice you'd like to convey to writers in the future?

A: Shall I give you an infallible little rule for verse? Here it is. When a thought is just and noble, something still remains to be done with it: see if the way you have expressed it in verse would be effective in prose: and if your verse, without the swing of the rhyme, seems to you to have a word too many--if there is the least defect in the construction--if a conjunction is forgotten--if, in brief, the right word is not used, or not used in the right place, you must then conclude that the jewel of your thought is not well set. Be quite sure that lines which have any one of these faults will never be learnt by heart, and never re-read: and the only good verses are those which one reads and remembers, in spite of oneself. There are many of this kind in your "Epistle" --lines which no one else in my generation could write at your age such as were written fifty years ago. (12)

Q: Any advice for man in general?

A: Put two men on the globe, and they will only call good, right, just, what will be good for them both. Put four, and they will only consider virtuous what suits them all: and if one of the four eats his neighbour's supper, or fights or kills him, he will certainly raise the others against him. And what is true of these four men is true of the universe. (13)

Therefore, teach men, not to persecute men: for, while a few sanctimonious humbugs are burning a few fanatics, the earth opens and swallows up all alike. (14)

Just like that, Monsieur Voltaire was swallowed up and returned from whence he came. I considered the state of the world today and saddened by our lack of progress read the following poem aloud:

FROM LOVE TO FRIENDSHIP

If you would have me love once more,
The blissful age of love restore;
From wine's free joys, and lovers' cares,
Relentless time, who no man spares,
Urges me quickly to retire,
And no more to such bliss aspire.
From such austerity exact,
Let's, if we can, some good extract;
Whose way of thinking with this age
Suits not, can ne'er be deemed a sage.
Let sprightly youth its follies gay,
Its follies amiable display;

Life to two moments is confined,
Let one to wisdom be consigned.
You sweet delusions of my mind,
Still to my ruling passion kind,
Which always brought a sure relief
To life's accurst companion, grief.
Will you forever from me fly,
And must I joyless, friendless die?
No mortal e'er resigns his breath
I see, without a double death;
Who loves, and is beloved no more,
His hapless fate may well deplore;
Life's loss may easily be borne,
Of love bereft man is forlorn.
'Twas thus those pleasures I lamented,
Which I so oft in youth repented;
My soul replete with soft desire,
Vainly regretted youthful fire.
But friendship then, celestial maid,
From heaven descended to my aid;
Less lively than the amorous flame,
Although her tenderness the same.
The charms of friendship I admired,
My soul was with new beauty fired;
I then made one in friendship's train,
But destitute of love, complain. (15)

Monsieur Voltaire's entire collection is worth reading but check these out and soon you'll want more!

Philosophical Dictionary
Candide
Micromegas
To The Queen of Hungary
Zadig
L'Ingenu
The Padlock

The Temple of Friendship
In Camp Before Philippsburg, July 3, 1734
On the Death of Adrienne Lecourvreur, a Celebrated Actress
The White Bull
The English Letters
The Ignorant Philosopher
The Henriad: A Poem
Critical Essays on Dramatic Poetry
Letters from M. de Voltaire to Friends
To a Lady Very Well Known to the Whole Town
Azolan
From Love to Friendship.

Adieu!
Cathy McGough
Your Interviewer of Legendary Writers From Beyond

ABOUT THE AUTHOR:

Multi-award winning author Cathy McGough
lives and writes in Oakville, Ontario, Canada,
with her husband, son and their two cats.
If you'd like to talk to Cathy please send her an email to:
cathy@cathymcgough.com.
She loves to hear from her readers.

ALSO BY:

FICTION

Everyone's Child

Ribby's Secret

The Umbrella and the Wind

Margaret's Revelation

Dandelion Wine (READERS' FAVOURITE BOOK AWARD FINALIST)

Plus Size Goddess

NON-FICTION

103 Fundraising Ideas For Parent Volunteers With Schools and Teams (3RD PLACE BEST REFERENCE 2016 METAMORPH PUBLISHING)

REFERENCES

INTRODUCTION

(1)
The Pilgrim's Progress, The Religious Tract Society, Bouverie St. and 65 St.
Paul's Churchyard, 1913.

CHAPTER I

(1)
As You Like It, Hodder and Stoughton, undated.
(2)
Song lyrics by Jim Morrison, L.A. Woman, 1971
(3)
Song lyrics by Jim Morrison, Waiting for the Sun, 1968.
(4)
Les Fleurs du Mal, The Casanova Society, London, 1925.

CHAPTER II

(1)
One Hundred and One Famous Poems, The Cable Company, Chicago, Illinois, 1924.
(2)
Tennyson, English Men of Letters, Macmillan, 1910.

(3)
Alfred, Lord Tennyson Letters, Toronto: Macmillan Company of Canada, 1929
(4)
Ibid
(5)
Bibliographies of Twelve Victorian Authors, The H.W. Wilson Comp., New York,
1936.
(6)
Tennyson, English Men of Letters, Macmillan, 1910
(7)
Ibid
(8)
One Hundred and One Famous Poems, The Cable Company, Chicago, Illinois, 1924.
(9)
An American Anthology, Houghton, Mifflin and Company, The Riverside Press,
Cambridge, 1900. .
(10)
British Poetry and Prose, Third Edition, Volume II, Houghton Mifflin Company,
Boston. 1938.
(11)
Song lyrics by Bono, All That You Can't Leave Behind, 2000.
(12)
Days With The Poets, London, Hodder & Stoughton, Percy Lund, Humphries
& Co. Ltd. Undated copy.
(13)
Ibid

CHAPTER III

(1)
An American Anthology, Houghton, Mifflin and Company, The Riverside Press,
Cambridge, 1900.
(2-5)
Edgar Allan Poe, Letters Till Now Unpublished, Lippincott, Philadelphia, 1925.
(6)
One Hundred and One Famous Poems, The Cable Company, Chicago, Illinois, 1924.
(7)
Edgar Allan Poe, Letters Till Now Unpublished, Lippincott, Philadelphia, 1925
(8)
Ibid
(9)
One Hundred and One Famous Poems, The Cable Company, Chicago, Illinois, 1924.
(10)
An American Anthology, Houghton, Mifflin and Company, The Riverside Press,
Cambridge, 1900.
(11)
Ibid.

CHAPTER IV

(1)
British Poetry and Prose, Third Edition, Volume II, Houghton Mifflin Company,
Boston. 1938.
(2)
Ibid
(3)
Shelley In England: New Facts and Letters from the Shel-

ley-Whitton Papers,
1917.
(4-6)
Days With The Poets, London Hodder & Stoughton, Percy Lund, Humphries &
Co. Ltd. Undated copy.
(7)
The English Poets In Pictures, Penns In The Rocks Press, William Collins of
London, 1941.
(8)
Ibid
(9)
Days With The Poets, London, Hodder and Stoughton, Percy Lund, Humphries &
Co. Ltd. Undated copy.
(10)
Ibid
(11)
British Poetry and Prose, Third Edition, Volume II, Houghton Mifflin Company,
Boston. 1938.
(12)
A Defence of Poetry, P. B. Shelley, 1840.
(13)
The Letters of Percy Bysshe Shelley, The Bodley Head, 1929
(14)
An Anthology of World Poetry, Cassell and Company Ltd., 1929.
(15)
Ibid
(16)
Essays and Letters by Percy Bysshe Shelley, Rhys, Ernest, undated.

(17)
British Poetry and Prose, Third Edition, Volume II, Houghton Mifflin Company,
Boston. 1938.
(18)
The Letters of Percy Bysshe Shelley, The Bodley Head, 1929
(19)
Ibid
(20)
A Defence of Poetry, P. B. Shelley, 1840.
(21)
British Poetry and Prose, Third Edition, Volume II, Houghton Mifflin Company,
Boston. 1938.

CHAPTER V

(1)
'No Thoroughfare', Christmas number of All The Year Round, 3 December 1867
(2)
Preface to My Lady's Money, Alan Sutton Publishing Company, 1890.
(3)
Wilkie Collins, June 1870, Preface to "Man and Wife" Peter Fenolon Collier,
Pub. Undated.
(4-7)
Introduction to "Hide and Seek, Oxford University Press, London, no date.
(8)
Preface to The First Edition of The Moonstone, 1868
(9)
Ibid
(10-12)
"No Name" Harper and Brothers, New York, 1873.

(13)
Little Novels, Chatto and Windus, Piccadilly, London, 1887.
(14)
"The Legacy of Cain", Donohue; Henneberry & Co., Chicago, undated edition
(15)
From Sea to Sea and Other Sketches, Letters of Travel, Vol. 1, Doubleday, Page
and Co., New York, 1925.
(16)
Little Novels, Chatto and Windus, Piccadilly, London, 1887.

CHAPTER VI

(1)
Memoir of Robert Burns, Frederick Warne and Co., Bedford Street, Strand,
London, undated
(2)
The "Chandos Classics", The Poetical Works of Robert Burns, Frederick Warne and
Co., Bedford Street, Strand, London, undated edition.
(3)
Memoir of Robert Burns, Frederick Warne and Co., Bedford Street, Strand,
London, dated
(4-15)
The "Chandos Classics", The Poetical Works of Robert Burns, Frederick Warne and
Co., Bedford Street, Strand, London, undated edition.

CHAPTER VII

(1)
Mark Twain's Letters, Harper, New York, 1917.
(2)
Paine, Albert Bigelow. Mark Twain: A Biography (New York:

Harper &
Brothers, 1912.)

(3)

Following The Equator, American Publishing Co., 1897.

(4)

Ibid

(5)

The Adventures of Tom Sawyer, Grosset & Dunlap, 1920.

(6)

The Innocents Abroad, H. H. Bancroft & American Pub. Co., San Francisco,
and Hartford, 1869

(7)

Letters of Mark Twain, Chatto & Windus, London, 1920.

(8)

Pudd'n'head Wilson, Chatto & Windus, 1926.

(9)

Ibid

(10)

Mark Twain wrote this in 1905, but it wasn't published until after his death.
It appeared in Harper's Monthly, November 1916. The same magazine had rejected
it previously.

(11)

Twain Letter to D. W. Bowser, 3/20/1880

(12)

Connecticut Yankee in King Arthur's Court, N.Y. Pocketbooks, 1948.

(13)

Letters of Mark Twain, Chatto & Windus, London, 1920.

(14)

The Celebrated Jumping Frog of Calaveras County and Other Sketches, C. H. Webb,
1867.

(15)
Letter to D.W. Bowser, March 20, 1880.
(16)
Harpers Monthly Magazine, 1909.

CHAPTER VIII
(1)
A Day with Samuel Taylor Coleridge, Hodder and Stoughton, London, 1885
(2)
Ibid
(3)
The Rime of the Ancient Mariner and Other Poems, Houghton Mifflin and Company,
Boston, 1931.
(4)
A Day with Samuel Taylor Coleridge, Hodder and Stoughton, London, 1885
(5)
Ibid
(6)
Ibid
(7)
Samuel Taylor Coleridge, Letters, Conversations and Recollections, Harper &
Bros., 1836.
(8)
A Day with Samuel Taylor Coleridge, Hodder and Stoughton, London, 1885.
(9)
Charles Lamb & The Lloyds: Newly Discovered Letters Of Lamb, Coleridge, The
Lloyds. Phila: Lippincott, 1899.
(10)
The Rime of the Ancient Mariner and Other Poems,

Houghton Mifflin and Company,
Boston, 1931.
(11)
Ibid
(12)
Ibid
(13)
A Day with Samuel Taylor Coleridge, Hodder and Stoughton, London, 1855.

CHAPTER IX

(1) The Writings of Nathaniel Hawthorne.
Boston and New York: Houghton, Mifflin and Company, 1900
(2)
The Scarlet Letter Preface, Ticknor, Reed and Fields, Boston: 1850.
(3-8)
Famous American Authors, Vail-Ballou Press, Inc., Binghamton, New York, 1933.
(9)
Living Biographies of Great Novelists, Garden City Publishing Co., Inc. 1943.
(10)
Ibid
(11)
Living Biographies of Great Novelists, Garden City Publishing Co., Inc. 1943
(12)
Ibid
(13)
Famous American Authors, Vail-Ballou Press, Inc., Binghamton, New York, 1933
(14)
Ibid

(15-19)
The Scarlet Letter Preface, Ticknor, Reed and Fields, Boston: 1850.
(20-22)
English Notebooks, Cambridge: Houghton, Mifflin and Company, 1889
(23-26)
Preface to The Blithedale Romance, E.P. Dutton & Co., 1925.
(27)
Passages from the English Notebooks of Nathaniel Hawthorne (1870)
(28)
Ibid
(29)
The Scarlet Letter, Ticknor, Reed and Fields, Boston: 1850
(30)
The Writings of Nathaniel Hawthorne. Boston and New York: Houghton, Mifflin and
Company, 1900

CHAPTER X
(1)
Stephen Leacock, Hellements of Hickonomics in Hiccoughs of Verse Done in our
Social Planning Mill (New York: Dodd, Mead, 1936
(2)
"Teaching School" The Boy I Left Behind Me, Doubleday, 1946.
(3)
Ibid
(4)
Ibid
(5)
Stephen Leacock, Hellements of Hickonomics in Hiccoughs

of Verse Done in our
Social Planning Mill (New York: Dodd, Mead, 1936

(6)

My Financial Career. Literary Lapses: A Book of Sketches. Montreal: Gazette
Printing Co., 1910.

(7-14)

"Teaching School" The Boy I Left Behind Me, Doubleday, 1946.

(15-17)

My Discovery of England: Dodd, Mead & Co. 1922.Ibid

CHAPTER XI

(1)

It Can Be Done, Poems of Inspiration, The Ryerson Press, Toronto, 1926.

(2-5)

Something of Myself (For My Friends Known and Unknown), Doubleday, Doran &
Co. Inc., 1937.

(6)

American Notes, Henry Altemus, Philadelphia, 1899.

(7)

Ibid

(8)

Rudyard Kipling's Verse, Hodder and Stoughton, London, 1928

(9)

A Diversity of Creatures, Letters of Travel 1892-1913, Doubleday, Page and Co.,
New York, 1925.

(10-12)

A Book of Words, Royal Academy Dinner speech, May 1906.

(13)

Something of Myself (For My Friends Known and Unknown),

Doubleday, Doran &
Co. Inc., 1937

(14)

Ibid

(15)

From Sea to Sea and Other Sketches, Letters of Travel, Vol. 1, Doubleday, Page and Co., New York, 1925.

CHAPTER XII

(1)

David Copperfield, Illustrated Collins School Classics, undated

(2)

Ibid

(3)

A Tale of Two Cities, New York: The MacMillan Company, 1921.

(4)

The Unpublished Letters of Charles Dickens, Halton & Truscott Smith, London, 1927.

(5)

The Letters of Charles Dickens, Chapman and Hall, London, 1880-82

(6)

The Life of Charles Dickens, T. B. Peterson & Brothers, Philadelphia, 1870.

(7-9)

Oliver Twist, F. M. Lupton, New York, 1895.

10)

David Copperfield, Illustrated Collins School Classics, undated

(11)

Ibid

(12)
A Tale of Two Cities, New York: The MacMillan Company, 1921.
(13-15)
American Notes for General Circulation, Chapman & Hall, London, 1910.
(16)
Letters and Speeches of Charles Dickens, Chapman & Hall, London, 1929.
(17)
Heart Throbs in Prose and Verse, Chappel Publishing Co. Ltd., 1905
(18)
Letters and Speeches of Charles Dickens, Chapman & Hall, London, 1929.

CHAPTER XIII

(1)
Dostoevsky Letters and Reminiscences, S. S. Koteliansky and J. Middleton Murry
translators. London, Chatto and Windus, 1923.
(2)
Ibid
(3)
Notes from Underground, The Short Novels of Dostoevsky, Dial Press, 1945
(4)
New Dostoevsky Letters, The Mandrake Press, London, undated edition.
(5-8)
Dostoevsky: A New Biography, Houghton Mifflin and Co., 1931.
(9)
The Insulted and the Humiliated Foreword, Moscow Publishers, Moscow, 1957

(10)
Dostoevsky: Letters and Reminiscences, Chatto and Windus, 1923.

(11)
The Possessed: The Heritage Press, New York, 1936.

(12)
Notes from Underground, The Short Novels of Dostoevsky, Dial Press, 1945

(13)
Letters and Reminiscences, Alfred A. Knopf, New York, 1923.

(14)
Fyodor Dostoevsky. Harrison of Paris, 1931.

(15)
New Dostoevsky Letters, The Mandrake Press, London, undated edition.

(16)
Fyodor Dostoevsky, SCM Press, London, 1948.

(17)
New Dostoevsky Letters, The Mandrake Press, London, undated edition.

(18)
Dostoevsky: A New Biography, Houghton Mifflin and Co., 1931

(19)
Dostoevsky speech given at Society of Friends of Russian Literature, August
1880. Recorded in The Diary of a Writer.

(20)
The Meek, The Eternal Husband and Other Stories, Macmillan, New York, 1923.

CHAPTER XIV

(1)
John Keats the Complete Poetical Works and Letters,

Houghton Mifflin, Boston,
1899.
(2-4)
John Keats His Life and Poetry, Macmillan and Co. Ltd., 1917
(5)
Letters of John Keats, Macmillan and Company, London, 1891.
(6)
John Keats the Complete Poetical Works and Letters, Houghton Mifflin, Boston,
1899.
(7-8)
Life, Letters and Literary Remains of John Keats, Edward Moxton, London, 1848.
(9)
John Keats His Life and Poetry, Macmillan and Co. Ltd., 1917
(10)
John Keats' Letters, 1817
(11)
John Keats His Life and Poetry, Macmillan and Co. Ltd., 1917
(12)
John Keats the Complete Poetical Works and Letters, Houghton Mifflin, Boston,
1899
(13)
Ibid
(14)
John Keats His Life and Poetry, Macmillan and Co. Ltd., 1917
(15)
John Keats the Complete Poetical Works and Letters, Houghton Mifflin, Boston,
1899.
(16)
John Keats the Letters and Papers, Bodley Head, 1914.

(17)
John Keats His Life and Poetry, Macmillan and Co. Ltd., 1917
(18)
Selections in English Literature, The Copp Clark and Co. Ltd., 1929.
(19)
Life, Letters and Literary Remains of John Keats, Edward Moxton, London, 1848.
(20)
John Keats the Complete Poetical Works and Letters, Houghton Mifflin, Boston,
1899.
(21)
Ibid

CHAPTER XV

(1)
Borrowings, Dodge Publishing Company, New York, 1899.
(2)
Poets' Homes, D. Lothrop Company, Boston, 1879.
(3)
Preface to Evangeline, Thomas Y Crowell and Co., New York and Boston, 1899.
(4-6)
Through the Year With Longfellow, De Wolfe, Fiske and Co., Boston, 1900.
(7)
Poets' Homes, D. Lothrop Company, Boston, 1879.
(8)
Longfellow Day By Day, Crowell, New York, 1906.
(9)
Ibid
(10)
An American Anthology, Houghton, Mifflin

and
Company, The Riverside Press, Cambridge, 1900.
(11)
Heart Throbs in Prose and Verse, Chapple Publishing Company Ltd., Boston,
Mass., 1905.
(12)
Longfellow Day By Day, Crowell, New York, 1906.
(13)
Poets' Homes, D. Lothrop Company, Boston, 1879.
(14)
Borrowings, Dodge Publishing Company, N.Y., 1889
(15)
Poets' Homes, D. Lothrop Company, Boston, 1879

CHAPTER XVI

(1)
A. B. "Banjo" Paterson, A Book of Verse, Angus and Robertson, Australia, 1990.
(2-4)
Happy Dispatches by A. B. Banjo Paterson, Lansdowne Press, 1934.
(5)
Reminiscences, Sydney Morning Herald, Feb. /March, 1939.
(6)
Ibid
(7)
Introduction to the Penguin Book of Australian Ballads.
(8)
The complete Poetry of A. B. "Banjo" Paterson, Harper Collins Publishers,
Australia, 1997.
(9)
Looking Backward, Sydney Morning Herald, 1941

(10-12)
The Magic of Verse, Angus and Robertson Ltd., 1970

CHAPTER XVII

(1)
Henry David Thoreau, Unpublished Poems, Bibliophile Society, Boston, 1907
(2-5)
Walden, Ticknor & Fields, Boston, 1854
(6)
Henry David Thoreau, Unpublished Poems, Bibliophile Society, Boston, 1907.
(7-10)
Walden, Ticknor & Fields, Boston, 1854
(11-14)
On the Duty of Civil Disobedience, Part 2.
(15)
Walden, Ticknor & Fields, Boston, 1854.
(16)
Ibid
(17)
An Anthology of World Poetry, Cassell and Company Ltd., 1929.
(18)
Walden, Ticknor & Fields, Boston, 1854
(18)
Ibid

CHAPTER XVIII

(1)
Letters and Journals of Lord Byron, John Murray, London, 1833.
(2)
The Letters of George Gordon Byron, Letter to William

Bankes, Southwell March
6, 1807.

(3)
Selections in English Literature, The Copp Clark and Co. Ltd., 1929.

(4)
Lord Byron's Journal Entry, November 14, 1813.

(5)
Byron letter to John Murray, Riavennia, July 30, 1821

(6)
Byron letter to Thomas Moore, Pisa, March 4, 1822

(7)
Letters and Journals of Lord Byron, John Murray, London, 1833

(8)
Lord Byron's Journal, Entry Nov. 17, 1813.

(9)
Poetry of Byron, Macmillan, London, 1881.

(10)
Lord Byron's Select Works, Charles Daly, London, 1836.

(11)
Childe Harold Introduction, London: Macmillan, 1904

(12)
Ibid

(13)
A Day With Byron, Hodder and Stoughton Ltd., undated

(14)
Lord Byron's Journal, Nov. 14, 1813.

(15)
Poetry of Byron, Macmillan, London, 1881.

(16)
Lord Byron's Journal, Nov. 14, 1813.

(17)
Lord Byron's Journal, Entry Nov. 17, 1813.

(18)
Lord Byron Letter to James Hogg, Albany, March 24, 1814.
(19)
Lord Byron's Journal Entry Oct. 15, 1821
(20-22)
Letters and Journals of Lord Byron, John Murray, London, 1833.
(23)
Childe Harold, London: Macmillan, 1904
(24-26)
Childe Harold Introduction, London: Macmillan, 1904
(27)
Lord Byron's Journal Entry, March 17, 1814
(28)
A Day With Byron, Hodder and Stoughton Ltd., undated.
(29)
Ibid
(30)
Lord Byron's Select Works, Charles Daly, London, 1836.

CHAPTER XIX

(1-8)
Les Fleurs du Mal, The Casanova Society, London, 1925.

CHAPTER XXI

(1)
The Best of All Possible Worlds: Romances And Tales By Voltaire, Vanguard Press
New York 1929
(2)
Toleration and Other Essays by Voltaire. Translated, with an Introduction, by
Joseph McCabe (New York: G.P. Putnam's Sons, 1912).
(3)
The Best Of All Possible Worlds: Romances And Tales By

Voltaire, Vanguard Press
New York 1929
(4)
Ibid
(5)
Darrow, Clarence S. Voltaire. A Lecture, [Girard, Kansas: Haldeman-Julius.
1925.
(6)
Voltaire The Writings of Voltaire NY: Wm.H. Wise, 1931
(7)
The Best Of All Possible Worlds: Romances And Tales By Voltaire, Vanguard Press
New York 1929
(8)
Darrow, Clarence S. Voltaire. A Lecture. [No.829 in the 'Little Blue Book'
series] Girard, Kansas.: Haldeman-Julius. 1925.
(9)
Letters concerning the English Nation. Westminster Press London 1926
(10)
Darrow, Clarence S. Voltaire. A Lecture, Girard, Kansas: Haldeman-Julius. 1925.
(11)
Ibid
(12-14)
Darrow, Clarence S. Voltaire. A Lecture, Girard, Kansas: Haldeman-Julius. 1925.
(15)
Selected Works of Voltaire, Watts and Co 1935.

www.ingramcontent.com/pod-product-compliance
Lightning Source LLC
Chambersburg PA
CBHW030813210726
48290CB00002B/568